To David

Enjoy my Story

Best Wishes

Fab

from Ashleigh

full english

From Ashleigh

foreword

If ever a player was fitting and worthy of a testimonial it's Mr Consistent Fabian Wilnis. A truly loyal servant, he was a model professional and outstanding defender during his years with Ipswich Town. I first became aware of his talent during my time as Manchester City manager. Mark Kennedy, our winger, was flying at the time and we expected him to have a field day. Not so. Fabian was that good – he marked him out of the game and completely nullified his threat.

It was then my great privilege to manage him when I took over at Portman Road. I took a liking to him from day one, from the minute I saw that big welcoming smile. He's a lovely guy – a real family man with a beautiful wife and children – and he was a terrific defender who always tried his best. He trained hard and, at another time, there's no doubt in my mind he would have been capped by Holland.

I didn't have any hesitation in playing him at right-back, left-back or centre-half and it never surprised me how easily he slotted into any of those roles. Fabian was always particularly good in a one-on-one situation. Whenever he found himself in that position, you'd always put your money on him to win. He was what I'd call a 'common sense' defender. He had a Dutch defender's knack of getting close to people. When he was a full-back, he was a master of stopping players getting crosses into the box and when he was a centre-half, he was so often in exactly the right place to block or prevent shots on goal.

Fabian was always the ultimate professional. He never had any weight issue (in fact, he still looks incredibly fit now) and from my point of view, as his manager, he didn't cause me a moment of trouble. There were never any histrionics if things weren't going his way. He just got on with the job in hand.

When I was approached about writing this foreword, I was asked if I had any recollections of him having particularly good games. The honest answer is no and that's a great compliment because he was consistent and reliable in every match. He set his standards that high.

Off the pitch, he's a lovely man who has well and truly earned his testimonial. There are many undeserved cases of players being granted them nowadays just because they're big names but that's certainly not the case for Fabian. It should be a wonderful day and occasion for him, especially as it's a local derby against Colchester United.

I hope he enjoys every minute of it and I wish him and his family the very best for the future.

Joe Royle

Fabian Wilnis experienced it all during his time at Portman Road. From Wembley and promotion to relegation and administration, his near decade with the club was nothing short of eventful. Who could forget the highs – the Premier League, Europe and goals against Manchester United and Norwich? Equally, there were lows – not least the unfortunate breakdown of his relationship with George Burley. This is the definitive account of recent Ipswich history, spoken from the heart of a Blues legend.

fabian wilnis

experience a truly honest account of Fab's last 10 years at ITFC

1 **2000**
Wembley wonders

2
Learning my trade

3 **98 99**
Pastures new

4 **99 00**
The only way is up

5 **00 01**
Living the dream

6 **01 02**
A clash of cultures

7 **02 03**
A change of boss

8 **03 04**
So near and yet so far

9 **04 05**
Deja vu

10 **05 06**
The end of an era

11 **06 07**
Jim takes the reins

12 **07 08**
All good things must
come to an end

13 **08 09**
From Blues to Grays

14 **09**
A year I'll never forget

15
Juilette's story

16
Looking to the future

acknowledgements

There are lots of people I'd like to thank, both for their help with this book and for their support and friendship during my time in England. In terms of the Full English, I'd like to mention Matt Plummer and Keith Suffling. Matt and myself became friends during my time at Ipswich, when he was reporting on the club for the Gazette in Colchester. Joining forces for this project has been a great experience and I thank him for relaying my thoughts and feelings so accurately. Keith has done the most brilliant job designing the book. So much dedication and creativity has gone into the layout and I thank him for his invaluable contribution and enthusiasm. Ipswich-wise, the most important people to thank are the fans – for their unswerving loyalty through the good times and the bad. They are wonderful supporters and I wish them every success and happiness. I'd also like to mention my three Town managers, George Burley, Joe Royle and Jim Magilton. George showed faith in me by bringing me to Portman Road and making this whole experience possible, Joe reignited my career after a sticky patch and Jim was a brilliant team-mate, captain and boss. He was also a driving force behind me being granted a testimonial.

In the last 12 months, I owe a huge debt of gratitude to my wonderful Fab10 committee - Duncan Foster, Mark Lomas, Adrian Horne, Dennis Tennial, Keith Suffling, Steve Flory, Steve Hayward-Jones and Mike Cooper. They've contributed so much towards making the events a success and I'm eternally thankful for their efforts. Likewise, Pam Davis has also been incredibly helpful. Andy Abbott and Tessa from the East Anglian Daily Times/Evening Star deserve a special mention for all their help in providing me with so many of the beautiful pictures in this book and I'm also very grateful to Fred and Catherina. They know why and their support has been much appreciated. Finally, I'd like to thank the most important people in my life – my family. Juliette, my wife, has been my best friend, rock and soul mate through the whole football adventure, by my side during the good times but especially the bad. She has always been the driving force behind me and I couldn't have done all this without her unconditional love and support. Yasmin, Jada and Kaylee, my beautiful girls, are my pride and joy and they were the ones who always cheered me up when I felt down after a bad result.

Best wishes,

Picture: copyright © Action Images, 2009 / John Marsh

full english

Hanging in the air - Tony Mowbray sends a
header goal-wards to get us back on level
terms before half-time.

Magic moment – Martijn Reuser's brilliant
goal sewed the game up and made our dream
a reality. We were Premier League footballers!

All together now - the boys and myself bask in the glory of our dramatic play-off success at Wembley.

wembley wonders

May 29th, 2000 – Wembley Stadium. The greatest day of my football life and the only place to begin my story. Ipswich Town's trip to the famous stadium for the Division One play-off final against Barnsley will always be ingrained in my memory. Not so much the game itself – I don't remember much apart from the goals – but for the tidal wave of emotion leading up to the day, then the sheer, unbridled joy and relief after our victory. It was a surreal, momentous and overwhelming feeling and certainly something I'm proud and thankful for.

To think Ipswich were a Premier League club again and that I was a Premier League footballer! It was almost too much to digest and little wonder myself and the boys celebrated as we did. I know I'll take those images and memories to my grave and I dare say it's the same for the other boys and thousands of loyal fans who were there to support us that day. The scene and atmosphere they created will forever be cemented in my recollections, starting from the minute we boarded our coach from the hotel to the stadium. As our police escort helped us snake along, the sights through the window were jaw dropping. By the time the Twin Towers were in sight, the view had become an explosion of people and colour - of Ipswich blue and Barnsley red. Our fans were singing and chanting, mouthing words of encouragement and giving us claps and thumbs-up. The view of Wembley Way was even more awe-inspiring – on one side perfect blue and the other dazzling red, as far as the eye could see. That's when the nerves kicked in. Proper nerves - not just the occasional flutter of butterflies. Our moment had arrived and the sight of those supporters – not to mention the endless rows of coaches parked as we got off our bus – was a timely reminder of what this day and game meant to so many people.

As myself and the other players made our way to the dressing room, the enormity of the occasion was sinking in. So far, the experience had been amazing and unforgettable – but we were there to do a job, for the club, the fans and for ourselves and our careers. Our dressing room was the one on the right and I can remember it vividly, as I can the mood among the lads. We had music on, as usual, in an attempt to chill and calm ourselves, but no one was listening. We couldn't stop thinking about the task in hand and the fact our moment had finally arrived. Johno (David Johnson) and Veno (Mark Venus) were the only players who were still loud and vocal, as they always were. Having said that, even Johno was

> "When the line-up was confirmed, my overpowering feelings were anger and disappointment. I was so gutted, deflated and sapped of energy."

full english

a bit more subdued than usual – probably because, leading up to the match, he hadn't been 100 percent fit. In his heart, he knew he shouldn't have started – but who could blame him for trying. I know I wouldn't have wanted to miss out.

Stepping out on to the lush, perfect Wembley surface focused our minds even more, if that were possible. It seemed like the longest walk ever, along the tunnel and then across the running track on to the pitch. The stadium was still empty at that point and, as we clustered in the centre circle, proudly donning our special Wembley suits (I hadn't heard of that tradition before and it seemed odd to have a brand new, tailor-made suit that I was only going to wear once), it was impossible not to look around and consider the history of the place – the FA Cup moments we've all grown up with, England highlights like 1966 and now our own precious milestone, given that this was the last domestic match to take place before the rebuild.

I'd never been there before and haven't since, but I know that as a little boy it was one ground above all others I wanted to play at. For any young lad growing up in Holland, it was a dream to play at the mighty Wembley. When I was still living at home, it seemed such a long way away. I'd watched concerts on TV of people like Madonna, Michael Jackson, Queen and the Live Aid gig. I also remember unforgettable football matches there, like in Euro '96 when England completely outplayed Holland to beat them 4-1. Now there I was, pacing across the legendary turf – preparing for perhaps the ultimate moment a professional footballer can experience.

By the time we'd got changed for our warm-up, the ground was filling fast. The buzz was extraordinary and all I wanted was for kick-off to arrive – the ensuing minutes seemed like an eternity.

I was sitting on one side of the dressing room next to Martijn Reuser and I can remember telling him that this would be our moment. We looked into each other's eyes and made a promise that whichever of us came off the bench first would make an impact straight away. I somehow felt so confident that I'd come on and play a part on this historic day for the club. I went to the bathroom and saw Marcus Stewart sitting on the floor near the showers, knees up with his head facing his lap. I wanted to say something but just left him there, because he was so focused and concentrating on what was about to happen.

Manager George Burley told us that these moments don't come along very often. For some it only happens once. For lucky ones twice, but hundreds and thousands of footballers never have the opportunity we were about to experience, so we had to enjoy the moment and rise to the occasion. He was right, of course, and for me it was the one and only time I experienced a play-off final. I knew we were a better team than Barnsley, because we'd already beaten them twice that season – 6-1 at home and 2-0 at Oakwell, thanks to goals from James Scowcroft and Stewy. However, the manager said that counted for nothing. We had to show the fans, the media and the whole watching nation that we could do it on the day. He said we had to stick to our principle of keeping the ball on the ground and use the full size of the massive Wembley pitch. He also said he had so much confidence in every single one of us that he couldn't see any other outcome than promotion to the Premier League.

The fact I wasn't in the starting line-up was a body blow. I'd slowly got used to the idea of not playing but didn't like it one bit. It was very frustrating and not least because I'd started the three games before our play-off semi-final second leg against

Bolton. I felt I'd played well in the first leg, too, and helped the team get a brilliant result. To then not play in the return match was a dreadful feeling. To be honest, I couldn't believe it. Jim Magilton's hat-trick – without doubt his best game for the club – secured our place at Wembley and my personal disappointment was replaced by excitement, passion and adrenaline. For a little while, anyway. In the days leading up to the final, my focus was entirely on earning a spot in the team. It was quite awkward as Burley had to make a straight choice between Gary Croft and myself and we were great mates. Then, in our final two sessions, I started fearing the worst. In both practice games, he went with Crofty and I couldn't help thinking 'please God, don't let this happen'.

With hindsight, I can see it was a tough decision for the manager but at the time I wasn't feeling so reasonable. When the line-up was confirmed, my overpowering feelings were anger and disappointment. I was so gutted, deflated and sapped of energy. I didn't sleep well the night before and laid chatting to Martijn. He was often used as a substitute but, as an attacking player, knew there was a very good chance he'd get a taste of the action. For me, as a defender, there was no guarantee, unless someone was injured or having a bad game. It was hard not to feel bitter, but I tried to keep it in perspective. I was genuinely happy for the club and know other people would have done anything to be in my shoes – just to be in with a chance of gracing Wembley.

Despite my disappointment, I can honestly say it didn't stop me feeling every bit as involved and part of the team as the others. Just before we went out, everyone wished each other good luck by screaming 'come on' and 'this is our day'. The overwhelming feeling was that, no matter what, we would not be beaten and there were loud cheers from everyone,

including the whole coaching and medical staff. After all that excitement and anticipation, we were finally ready.

As the teams headed out on to the pitch – we were led out by Burley and the injured Scowie – a deafening wall of noise filled our eardrums. I'll never forget it and even now, nine years on, it makes the hairs on the back of my neck stand on end. We had the Town fans behind us as we emerged and I truly believe that gave us a psychological advantage – mentally we were already ahead. Robbie Williams' brilliant Let Me Entertain You (a perfect choice) belted out of the Tannoy and the explosion of noise was phenomenal. My body was flooded with adrenaline and I was covered in goose bumps – I defy anyone to feel differently, unless they're made of stone.

It was impossible to ask for more. The setting was perfect and, after Matt Holland introduced each of us to the dignitaries, I took my place on the bench – ready to kick, chase and scrap for every ball when I got my chance. It was an unforgettable day which I'll cherish forever. However, as I said earlier, my memories of the game itself are vague to say the least. It was a bit of a blur but I know Richard Wright's very unfortunate early own goal – a long-range shot came down off the bar, hit him and went in – sent a wave of nerves pulsing through my body. It was unbelievable – but there was still a long, long way to go. Anything could happen, but my fears got worse when Johno – our leading scorer for the previous three seasons – had to come off after 22 minutes when we were losing 1-0. The last thing we wanted was to replace our top striker so early in the game. He'd been struggling throughout the week leading up to the final and now he couldn't even move because it was so painful. Bam Bam (Richard Naylor) came on to replace him.

full english

Whether we played well or not I honestly couldn't say but we were level by the break. From Jim's corner, the awesome Tony Mowbray scored our goal, rising above everyone and hanging in the air to head us back into the contest. The half-time whistle went and I can remember staying on the pitch to kick a few balls with the other subs, Martijn, Wayne Brown and goalkeeper Keith Branagan. While we were out there, I had another good look round and soaked up the view. It was mesmerising to see a sold-out Wembley divided in the middle by Ipswich blue and Barnsley red. It was such a hot day and I stood there looking for my family and friends. I never

"Having only just come on, I had the freshest legs on the pitch and motored over to pounce on him. I was first on the scene but the others soon arrived at the party. What a feeling."

wanted the day to end. It was so beautiful and just thinking about it puts a smile on my face. As I was waving to my loved ones in the stand (after looking for nearly ten minutes I still couldn't spot my best friend Rene, who had come over from Holland) I noticed the players emerging for the second half. I wondered what the manager had said to them in the dressing room.

Bam Bam nicked the ball past the Barnsley goalkeeper to put us in front just after the restart and then, when Stewy made it 3-1, we dared to dream. I knew we could do it. Barnsley's Craig Hignett fired them back into contention with 12 minutes left and

that made for a scary finale. On one hand, if we scored again the match was over. On the other, if they got the next goal they'd have the confidence and momentum heading into extra time.

Thankfully, I was to get a chance to have a say in that outcome. With just two minutes left, Jermaine Wright took a knock. Like a vulture circling and ready to pounce, I leapt out of my seat. I ripped off my tracksuit top and, in a flash, was ready for my big moment – the precious few seconds I would tell my grandchildren about. I'd been praying to get on and, when Burley looked round to consider his options, the sight of me champing at the bit gave him no option. I honestly think I made the substitution for him. He duly gave me the nod and I was on. Within seconds, a long ball was pumped forward to Martijn. Everything seemed to happen in slow motion as my great friend and room-mate took the ball in his stride, then lashed it home for 4-2. Cue wild celebrations – not least from me. Having only just come on, I had the freshest legs on the pitch and motored over to pounce on him. I was first on the scene but the others soon arrived at the party. What a feeling.

Then the referee put the whistle to his lips and it was the most unbelievable sensation. The adrenaline starts to pump just talking about it. We were drunk with joy, as were our fans, and one of the first things I wanted to do was pick out my family in the crowd. It wasn't easy but there, among the masses, were my wife Juliette, little girl Yasmin and niece Serah (both four). They were waving at me and I was furiously motioning back at them. It was very special and picking out so many faces – all as euphoric as each other – was such a thrill.

Next it was time to climb those famous steps up to the Royal Box. Matt led the way and I screamed with delight when he lifted the trophy above his head.

Above: That's my boy - an ecstatic George Burley congratulates my fellow Dutchman Martijn Reuser after his heroics at Wembley.

Left: What a beauty – skipper Matt Holland proudly parades our magnificent silverware.

The emotional roller coaster was over and it was finally all about excitement and partying rather than ups and downs. By the time we got back down on the pitch, most of us were wearing hats, scarves or wigs donated by the fans – or a combination of all three. They made for some great pictures. I've got a brilliant one of me and Jim, arm in arm, and another with Stewy – minus his shorts, which he'd hurled to the fans. We did a lap of honour and Martijn and myself were last off the pitch. We milked it for all it was worth and I couldn't stop looking at the supporters and giant scoreboard, which flashed up messages of congratulations.

Back in the dressing room it was time to get wet. The bubbly was out and everyone was in for a drenching – not least Burley, whose previously immaculate suit was soon saturated. Everyone was singing and bouncing up and down. No wonder we made it last as long as possible. Finally, after wrapping up the party and doing our various interviews with the media, it was time to start the journey home – the longest drive I've ever experienced.

Getting from Wembley around the M25 wasn't too bad, but the trek up the A12 was the complete reverse. There were Town fans in cars and coaches everywhere and the volume of traffic made for a snail-like journey. Not that we minded. It was wonderful seeing all the faces pressed up against the windows, clapping and saluting our achievements. Lots of fans had gathered on the various bridges and there were flags and banners draped everywhere. I saw people screaming, dancing and singing right in front of our coach and that's when it really

full english

Party time – Jim Magilton and myself milk our big moment in front of the jubilant Town fans.

room. It was the first and only time I've really let myself go during my time at Ipswich. Initially, the whole squad stayed together at a special party at the Suffolk Showground but then a few of us moved on to Hollywood nightclub. I say a few of us but the only person I definitely remember being with me was Martijn. What a night we had. I didn't spend a single penny as people were buying us drinks all night and I got more and more drenched as ecstatic fans threw beer all over us. Grown men were crying as emotion – and alcohol – got the better of them. It was a very special, drunken night and well worth the excruciating hangover. Not that I thought it at the time, waking up in my sodden clothes and barely able to move.

A couple of days later we had an open-top bus tour of Ipswich, starting at Portman Road. It blew my mind to see that so many people had turned out to support us and I'll always treasure my photos and video camera footage. The streets were jam-packed and the slow drive to the town hall seemed to take an age. When we finally got there, up on to the balcony, we had our own individual moments in the spotlight. Each of the lads had an opportunity to say something as a microphone was passed round and, when Jim handed it to me, the only thing I could think to say was 'I love you all'. It was great fun.

That night we had a huge club party, including the various wives and girlfriends, so you could say we savoured the moment for all it was worth - and why not. Playing a part in getting Ipswich back in the Premier League was an extremely proud, privileged thing for me. Everyone knew about the achievements of the team that won the FA Cup in 1978 and UEFA Cup in 1981. Now a side I was part of had created a whole new chapter of history, a lasting legacy for the future generations of supporters. We had every reason to revel in the moment.

hit me what we'd done to their lives and how much it meant to those fans. It was truly a joy to share the moment with so many of them and when we finally arrived back at Portman Road there were more supporters everywhere. It was time to continue the party in more familiar surroundings.

In anticipation of a big night, Martijn and myself had booked into Ipswich's Novotel. Juliette was heavily pregnant with our second daughter, Jada, and she knew it was the sensible thing to do. She couldn't join us, obviously, and knew I might struggle to get home! She was right – I haven't got any memory whatsoever of getting back to my hotel

2

learning my trade

The size of our achievement, coupled with the euphoria of the moment, seemed a million miles from my early days in the game, when I was learning my trade back home in Holland. Playing football has always been part of my life, right from the start. As soon as I was old enough to walk, I started kicking a ball and there was nothing I enjoyed more than a game with my three older brothers, Kenneth, Brayen and Carlo. As the years rolled by, we'd spend hours together and, in that kind of football-mad environment, it was no surprise I became so passionate about the game.

Home comforts – my three brothers and me enjoyed nothing more than a game of football together.

When I was six, I joined my first youth team, a side called VV NOC. It will surprise people to know that for my first two or three years I was a goalkeeper. I was actually quite good but, within time, I started getting bored. We'd have games when we were so on top and I was stuck back between the posts, a virtual (and very frustrated) spectator. That wasn't for me. I wanted a taste of the action and in my spare time, when I was playing with my brothers, I was always an outfield player. Naturally, most young footballers want to be a striker, with the glory of scoring lots of goals, and I was no different. It was not a surprise, then, that I soon adopted that position, consigning my brief spell as a shot-stopper to the history books.

NOC was about 45 minutes away by bus, which, for a young lad, was quite a journey at the time. So, when I was 11, I experienced my first taste of the 'transfer market' by moving to a side closer to home, called YVV de Zwervers. It was actually a pivotal moment for me as, very soon after, I was the subject of some interest from mighty Feyenoord. For me, as a huge fan of the club, that felt amazing. We lived about 500 yards from the ground and my dad, Robert, was a steward there. He showed me the stadium – a jaw-dropping experience for a young fan with stars in his eyes - and he always made sure I got a good spot at the front of the main stand for all their home games.

Those childhood days were brilliant. It felt so special and now, at the age of 11, my boyhood heroes had approached me. I couldn't believe it. Sadly, the dream was over before it started. After having trials, Feyenoord decided I wasn't good enough and to say I was disappointed would be an understatement. I

Learning my trade – these images bring back memories of my early days playing for NAC Breda and De Graafschap.

was absolutely heartbroken, although looking back they were probably right – the opportunity had come too soon and I wasn't ready.

I spent four years with de Zwervers before another big opportunity presented itself, when I was 15. Sparta Rotterdam came along and then, ironically, there was more interest from Feyenoord. It was a tough call but I decided on Sparta. I figured that if I wasn't good enough for Feyenoord the first time then why should anything be different now? Not only that, Sparta were offering me something concrete, whereas Feyenoord simply invited me back for another trial. If it didn't work out, I'd be back to square one and would have kicked myself for missing such an opportunity. Sparta became my home for the next four years, until I was 19. I developed through their academy and then made my way into their senior team (which means something different in Holland. In English football, the senior team refers to the first team. Back home, the senior side is another stepping-stone on the way up).

It was a great time for me off the pitch, too, because it was during my Sparta days that I first met Juliette. She wasn't into football at all. She didn't understand anything about it and never came to watch me play. Then, one day, one of my friends said she should get along to a game and, reluctantly, she came and watched her first ever match. It was a cup final, which we lost, and afterwards she couldn't understand what all the fuss was about. Thankfully, her opinion soon changed (just as well, given that her life has been dominated by football ever since). She learnt the rules and soon became quite a fan, regularly shouting and screaming from the stands.

Things were going well and, although still only a semi-professional, my dream of making it was still alive and burning. My game was improving and developing all the time and I must have been getting a decent reputation, because within time I heard of some interest in me from NAC Breda. Apparently, they wanted me for their reserves, which would have been another step up.

A move duly followed and, within six or seven months with their reserves, I was invited to start training with the first team. All this time, ever since retiring my goalkeeping gloves, I'd been playing as a striker but my new club had more than enough front men, so I was asked how I'd feel about operating on the right of midfield. I was happy to give it a go and ended up spending a whole season there. To be honest, I took to it like a duck to water. Back then, I was really quick (hard to believe now) and used to love taking on defenders and getting crosses into the box. I think I had more assists that season than during the rest of my career put together.

One day, we came up against a team called VVV Venlo and they had the quickest winger in the whole league, an African player called Tijani Babangida. As I was the fastest player in our team, the manager asked me to go up against him as a left-back. I couldn't believe it. Not only had I never played as a full-back before, I'd never been on the left (the only position I've never played in is central midfield). Thankfully, the gamble worked. I had one of my best games for the club and completely nullified Babangida's threat. I kept up with him, in terms of pace, and not once did he get past me. At one point he got so frustrated he swapped wings, so I shifted over to right-back and continued to mark him out of the game.

Afterwards I was buzzing and the manager was impressed. I started playing more games as a full-back and we finished that season by getting promoted. Left-back was to become my new spot

full english

Pierre van Hooydonk has just scored for Nac Breda.

and I spent the next five years in that position, constantly working to improve my left foot. Every time I kicked a ball in training I'd try and use it. Sometimes I'd just kick the ball against a wall, always with my left foot of course, and in my third or fourth season I was honoured to be named player of the year.

NAC offered me a new deal when my contract expired after five years but, to be honest, it wasn't great. I felt it was derisory - peanuts. I'd been

a regular in their side and felt a bit hurt that they weren't prepared to offer more to keep one of their main players. Around the same time, De Graafschap were looking for a right-back. I was approached by their manager, a brilliant man called Frits Korbach, and it turned out they were prepared to offer me twice as much as NAC. It was an easy decision to make and I was soon on the move to another club.

Korbach turned out to be such an eccentric character. He was incredibly loyal to his players

Sharing the moment – as you can see, we had some great times together and there was nothing I loved more than celebrating goals.

and never once criticised them in public. When it came to speaking to officials or the press, though, he couldn't stop swearing and had a mouth like a sewer. Whatever the weather, even when it was freezing cold, he always wore shorts for training but when it came to looking smart and wearing a suit, he never wore socks. My other main memories are of him smoking big cigars during every game and wearing glasses that sat on the end of his nose, so he was constantly switching from looking through them to over them.

My first year with De Graafschap reminds me of that wonderful year at Ipswich, when we finished fifth in the Premier League. At one point we were second in the Dutch top flight, but sadly couldn't maintain it and had a little wobble after Christmas.

Like at Ipswich, the camaraderie between the players was excellent. Korbach had a new

joke to share with us every day and, as a squad of players, we had so many meals and nights out together. We used to hang out, spend time at each other's houses and the wives and girlfriends all got on brilliantly, too, so it was a happy time. In terms of atmosphere, it was the best I experienced in Holland.

Moving to De Graafschap was great for me football-wise but it was also the start of a new and exciting adventure for Juliette and myself. It was two hours away from Rotterdam, so for the first time in our lives we were leaving all our family and friends behind. We moved to a place called Doetinchem, right next to the German border in the east of Holland (we used to drive over the border to get cheap petrol). Not only that, Yasmin was a newborn baby at the time so we were experiencing our first taste of parenthood, too.

In my second season, I was crowned player of the year (keeping up my run of having won the award at each of my clubs) and then, in the summer of 1998, there was some interest in me from another Dutch side, AZ Alkmaar. I was keen to keep my options open so Juliette, my agent and myself had talks with them but a fee and personal terms couldn't be agreed, so I stayed at De Graafschap. I'm a big believer in fate and, looking back, think the move didn't happen for a reason because six months later I was on my way to Ipswich. Had I moved on, it's very unlikely I'd have got my dream move to England. Likewise, De Graafschap offered me a new three-year deal and I never signed that because of the interest from Portman Road. Had I put pen to paper, there probably would have been a clause meaning any other clubs would have had to fork out four or five times as much as the £200,000 paid by Ipswich. That, understandably, would have

full english

put them off and things might have worked out so differently – I might never have got my chance in England.

Looking back, I've got so many happy memories of my time learning the game in Holland. It was a real learning curve, both on the pitch and off it. People may have a pre-conceived idea that being a footballer is all about glamour and luxury, but my early experiences were the exact opposite. During my first seasons at Breda, I was only semi-professional so was leaving home first thing in the morning to attend a college course in engineering. I had to travel by train from my home in Rotterdam to the Hague, then get back for training in the afternoons and evenings. The first-team session started at 3.30pm and then the reserves trained at 6pm. It made for an absolutely exhausting day and getting back for the afternoons, especially, was always such a manic rush.

It was so stressful because I wanted to do well with my football and studying, but soon realised something had to give. I never had any energy for my homework or essays and I'd set off in the mornings with my books and pads in one bag and my kit in another. Sometimes I'd slump into a seat on the train and the movement as we rumbled along would send me off to sleep. I couldn't go on like that so had a chat with my mum and decided I had to choose between football and studying. It was a tough one to call but mum, Helen (a huge Feyenoord fan, I can see her now screaming and jumping around when they're live on telly!) made a great call and suggested I gave football a go for a year. She said I could always go back to my studies, whereas I might always regret it if I let the opportunity to play pass me by. Of course, it turned out to be very sensible advice, although I always had it in my head that one day I'd finish my education.

2

The big irony is that it had never been my intention to become a professional footballer. It was not my goal or dream, much as I enjoyed playing as a kid. In terms of making a living out of the game, it just happened and was something I grew into. Nowadays, because of the financial rewards, it seems lads are desperate to get a break and make lots of money, but back in my early days I only ever saw it as a hobby. My main incentive was a love of the game and, although football became my profession, that continued throughout my playing days.

During my time at Breda, soon after signing my first professional contract, I moved out of home and bought a little one-bedroom flat with Juliette. That was a real eye-opener in terms of the real world. At home, mum never asked for any housekeeping money because she knew my finances were tight. Now, I suddenly had to worry about bills and it was a real shock to the system. My wage was very ordinary back then and 50 percent was taxed straight away, with another ten percent automatically going into a pension fund. So in terms of actual income, we had to live off 40 percent of my salary.

For the first couple of years we really struggled. We couldn't afford hardly any new clothes and, as far as groceries went, we lived off the basics. It was a hard life but we managed and it made us stronger, although we were still relying on our family to some extent. On a Monday, we'd eat with Juliette's parents, on a Tuesday we'd scrounge a meal from mine, on a Thursday we'd see my brother and on a Sunday we'd see her sister! So we only had to fend for ourselves three nights a week.

In all honesty, it was the only way we could make ends meet and, although we might not have thought it at the time, it was great because it taught us how to survive. That's why we never take anything for granted now. As far as I'm concerned, I've worked really hard to get to where I am today but at times it was a real struggle and I'll never forget that. In terms of money worries, even worse was to come. When little Yasmin arrived, we had to move out of our flat into a house so then had a much bigger mortgage to contend with, not to mention the huge expense of catering for a newborn baby. We had to buy a bigger car, so we could get around as a family, and a lot of sacrifices had to made along the way.

We were always happy, though, and when Yasmin was 18 months old, in June 1998 (six months before my move to Ipswich), Juliette and myself got married in the Dominican Republic. We didn't tell anyone (I don't think I'd have survived if my friends had been able to give me a stag night). It was a very personal thing and just the way we wanted to do it, so the three of us jetted off and then, on the morning of the big day, we sent out letters inviting people to a big party to be held a month later. It was the most perfect wedding in the most beautiful of settings. The ceremony took place at 5pm, when the fierce afternoon heat was dwindling, and, after such a financial struggle, it finally seemed like we'd arrived.

I always thought my playing career would be over by the time I was 30. In Holland, that's the norm. When a player hits that milestone they're suddenly considered old, past it and over the hill. In England, however, a much kinder and more sympathetic word is used and a player is referred to as being 'experienced'. And far from my career coming to an end, it was effectively only just beginning.

full english

pastures new

A new chapter of my career – the best, longest and happiest - was about to unfold at Ipswich and those first few days will always be imprinted in my mind, not least because everything happened so quickly. From going about my day-to-day business in Holland, it was literally just a matter of days before my life was turned upside down and I was running out for my Town debut against Grimsby.

I first learnt of the club's interest through fellow Dutchman and Ipswich's European scout Romeo Zondervan. He told me they were on the lookout for someone new to replace Mauricio Taricco, who had joined Spurs, and that the club were stepping up their search in the wake of a disappointing home defeat against Barnsley. A young lad called John Kennedy had been playing as one of the full-backs but was raw and lacked experience – apparently Burley wanted someone to go straight into his first team. He was after a right wing-back and, although I was playing as a full-back at the time, I've always enjoyed attacking and getting forward and hoped I would fit the bill.

Zondervan told me Burley was coming over to watch me play the next weekend against AZ Alkmaar (Town were playing Sheffield United on the Sunday, as luck would have it) and I was instantly up for the challenge of proving myself. There were a few butterflies, obviously, because I knew it would be a dream come true to play in England, but I wasn't particularly nervous – just determined to do well and impress my potential new boss.

I absolutely ran my socks off. I got up and down the right-hand side and my chances were boosted by a strange quirk of fate, when our right-sided midfielder got sent off after just 20 minutes. We were down to ten men for the next 70. That left three in the middle but we didn't change our shape, which meant no one was playing in front of me. That, as it turned out, was ideal because it gave me a perfect opportunity to showcase my talent. I virtually had the right flank to myself and Burley could see I was capable and had sufficient energy levels to do a job for him. I was certainly very pleased with and confident in my performance, even though we lost 1-0.

Burley must have been convinced because on the Monday I got another call from Zondervan, telling me I was invited over to watch Ipswich's Boxing Day match at home to Portsmouth, and I sensed something exciting was about to happen as Juliette and I made the hop over the North Sea. If I'm honest, I was sold as soon as I arrived. The ground, the facilities, the people, the atmosphere – it was incredible and very special. Portman Road seemed like a typical English stadium and I remember being so impressed with the way people got behind the team, screaming and shouting. I wasn't used to it because although the atmosphere is good at big games back home, it's nothing compared to what I experienced that day. Certainly not in terms of passion and noise levels and I knew from that moment – if I didn't already – that I wanted to play my football in front of these people.

I met Burley for the first time before the game and he gave me a quick tour of the stadium, then took me to his office and told me exactly what

Dressed for success – posing in an Ipswich kit for my very first press conference, I'm ready to embark on my new life in England.

I wanted to hear – that he wanted to sign me. I also met chairman David Sheepshanks and it was impossible not to be impressed by both of them, given their passion, ambition and devotion for Ipswich. I was also taken aback by the history of the club. Anyone who's been lucky enough to walk round the corridors of Portman Road will have seen the vast array of pictures and newspaper cuttings which grace every wall. The club are obviously very proud of their heritage and rightly so. It was certainly an eye-opener for me, in terms of what a special club I was joining. I'd always been aware of Ipswich. I knew they'd won the FA Cup and UEFA Cup and I knew they'd had some famous Dutch players down the years, most notably Arnold Muhren and Frans Thijssen, but I didn't fully appreciate the scale of their successes and achievements - until then.

Although I was about to earn more than I had in Holland, my decision to join was never about money. It was purely about football – a chance to experience a whole new adventure in a different country at one of the best-known English clubs. It also meant a chance to improve my English, which appealed to me. I was playing in the Dutch Premier League so in some ways I was about to make a backwards step into a lesser division, but

"If I'm honest, I was sold as soon as I arrived. The ground, the facilities, the people, the atmosphere – it was incredible and very special. Portman Road seemed like a typical English stadium and I remember being so impressed with the way people got behind the team, screaming and shouting."

full english

Press gang – I was relieved to get to the end of my first press conference, although it was good to be joined on the podium by George Burley and David Sheepshanks.

for me it never felt like that. It felt like a giant leap forward because I was about to play for a bigger club, with a bigger stadium and fan base. Town and De Graafschap agreed a fee of £200,000 and I eventually put pen to paper on a three-and-a-half year deal. I never actually expected to stay that long (let alone nearly ten years). Footballers generally move on in less time than that and I was probably anticipating two to two-and-a-half years at Portman Road.

As I said, everything happened so quickly in terms of me being spotted to signing on the dotted line. The game in Holland was the final one before the Dutch winter break so I went from being set for a rest to the prospect of a whole new life and culture in England. It was a thrilling opportunity – one I was determined to grab with both hands – but on a personal level there was so much to sort out. People may not realise that kind of thing when they contemplate a footballer moving from club to club, from one location to the next and, in this instance, to a whole new country. As a footballing decision, it was very easy and didn't require a lot of thinking

time. I was playing top-flight football in Holland but it would undoubtedly be a great career move for me to experience life in England. It represented an exciting new challenge.

I still had my family to consider though, because there was Juliette and Yasmin (then coming up to three) to take into account. We had to sell our house, make arrangements at a new nursery and get lots of other things straight before we could up sticks and leave Holland (Juliette will tell you more later in the book). Having said that, it was still quite a straightforward decision. There was a bit of sadness at leaving home but to a large extent it was washed away by our genuine and shared excitement.

Juliette and Yasmin stayed behind for the first three months to get everything sorted while I travelled to Ipswich to meet my new team-mates. My first taste of the action was a reserve fixture at Portman Road, especially arranged for my benefit, but the strange thing is that I don't remember anything about it, apart from the fact I came off after about an hour. It was my very first appearance in a

Riding a tackle – here I am enjoying one of my first tastes of the English game.

Town strip but I couldn't tell you who we played or what the score was. That and the first couple of training sessions were certainly nerve-racking experiences, as you'd expect in day one of any new job. I didn't know what to expect but was determined to try my hardest and enjoy the experience of playing on the surprisingly immaculate training pitches. I was used to bobbly ones shared with other teams, so this was new to me and very impressive.

What surprised me most on my first day was the loud music in the dressing room. You could hear booming speakers long before you walked through the door. Kieron Dyer and David Johnson were the DJs and always looked after the CDs (most of which contained heavy garage). In Holland, we also used to listen to music but only on the radio and only half as loud. We never had it on on a match day. Every manager I played under in Holland always preferred peace and quiet so the players could fully focus and prepare themselves in a tranquil environment. They would certainly be in for a shock if they came over to England.

Here, it's quite normal to have music blasting out and my first impression of the dressing room on a match day was that I was in the wrong place – it felt like I was in a nightclub. Rather than looking like a group of professionals preparing for a match, people were singing, dancing, shaking their heads, taking the mickey out of each other and there were others even having a bath (that was also something I'd never seen before). I sat there in a corner watching in a state of shock. I thought 'this surely can't be right, we'll get hammered because these so-called players, my new colleagues, will never be switched on'.

In reality, I couldn't have been more wrong. The boys clicked from the first whistle and were so alert, sharp and focused. The game was 100 miles an hour for 90 minutes. It surprised me how much I started to like the pre-match music ritual. Back home, dressing rooms can be like a morgue when you're getting yourself ready for kick-off and time seems to drag. Here, the minutes fly by and, before you know it, it's time to play. Nowadays, I can't start a match without having listened to some heavy tunes in the dressing room, either on a stereo or my iPod. It's funny how your mindset changes.

"Town and De Graafschap agreed a fee of £200,000 and I eventually put pen to paper on a three-and-a-half year deal. I never actually expected to stay that long (let alone nearly ten years)."

full english

For the first three months I stayed at the Novotel hotel in Ipswich. My agent was with me for a few days and it was at that time he introduced me to a word I was soon to get very familiar with – gaffer. I'd never heard it before and didn't have a clue what it meant. It sounded more like an insult to me and I half wondered whether he was playing a little trick, because he wanted me to say it to Burley and then everyone would laugh. I'd only ever come across the words 'boss' and 'trainer' back home, so decided to hedge my bets and wait for other players to say it first. As you can imagine, it didn't take long for that to happen.

Something that worked against me during those early days was my lack of English. I'd studied it at school but it was only very average at best. I could watch English TV and get by when people spoke very slowly, but there were such a variety of accents in the dressing room and everyone seemed to speak so quickly. I couldn't exactly stop my team-mates during a training match and ask them to repeat themselves. I also had huge problems understanding Burley. He's obviously got a strong Scottish accent and seemed to speak so fast. I really had to concentrate to try and understand.

The biggest problem I had in terms of communication problems came during my very first press conference, the one specially arranged to unveil me as a new player. It took place on the same day I signed my contract and, as far as I was concerned, was an absolute nightmare. I was so nervous and kept stuttering – I didn't know how to respond to some of the questions. Some of the others I didn't understand at all. The only saving grace was that I had Burley and Mr Sheepshanks either side of me and they tried to help as much as possible. Even so, it was undoubtedly the most nerve-racking aspect of joining. When I play football or train, I'm very much in my comfort zone. Here, I was like a fish out of water and to say I was glad when it was over would be an understatement.

As for the players, they were a genuinely great bunch - very welcoming and friendly. Kieron Dyer shone as one of the most talented, although for someone that young he was so loud and undoubtedly the biggest mickey-taker. He was obviously something special, with quick feet, extraordinary pace and so much skill. Richard Wright was the other player who stood out. He was still a young goalkeeper but exceptionally talented and like a cat in the way he threw himself around to make saves. He had amazing reflexes. David Johnson and Mark Venus were real characters, as I've already mentioned, and so too was Jason Cundy.

Overall I couldn't help but be impressed by the quality of the squad. Johno was a strange one in that – being brutally honest – he didn't really impress me in that first training session. He was so small and didn't strike me as anything special. When I got to know him and started playing regularly with him, though, I completely changed my opinion. He was so quick and clinical, especially with his left foot, and his goals were an essential part of the success we shared in the next season or two.

Veno was loud and always up for a laugh, but he was also very intelligent and sensible. He had an opinion on absolutely everything and was razor-sharp and articulate. He often managed to goad Burley into a debate on something or other and I remember them wiling away many a long coach journey with some interesting, meaty discussions.

He certainly wasn't shy when it came to confrontation but he kept his feet on the ground. He wasn't your stereotypical flash footballer – you could tell that from the car he drove. While others prided themselves on their top-of-the-range motors, Veno kept faith in his old, trusty set of wheels – and justified it by saying it meant he didn't have to keep the car clean and tidy. Quite honestly, I've never seen or travelled in such a messy car in my life. We used to get changed at Portman Road, then drive up to the training ground at Bent Lane. One day Veno offered me a lift but it took ages to shift all the empty food wrappers, drink cartons and other assembled rubbish. Veno adopted an 'if it ain't broke don't fix it' attitude and I suppose that made sense.

Then, of course, we had the 'thinker' Tony Mowbray. On every away trip, he was always reading a book or autobiography or even a coaching manual. He was so calm, on and off the pitch, and people like myself could learn so much from him. I

certainly did in the year and a half I played with him. He's exactly the same now he's a manager and I see him as my big example and inspiration. If ever I follow the same path, or take up a coaching job, I'd love to be like him and seen in the same light.

I was quite happy with how I adapted in the first few training sessions. The pace was a big surprise – everything is more patient and methodical back home – but I fitted in well and was never out of my depth. The lads dished out a yellow bib to whoever they thought was the worst trainer every Friday and, I'm pleased to say, it never came my way. That had to be a good sign. For my money, the best trainer at the club was Jamie Clapham. His fitness levels were extraordinary, superior to anyone else at the club at that time, and he could run and run. I thought I was fit but was a slouch in comparison.

I was fortunate in that there were two other Dutch lads in the camp at that time – Bobby Petta and Marco Holster. Marco was actually my first room-mate, albeit briefly, and then I started sharing with Micky Stockwell. It took a while to get used to staying in a hotel before every away game, even if it was somewhere nearby like Norwich or London. In Holland, we never travelled the day before a game but always on the day of the match itself. Then again, given the size of the country, our furthest away match over there was only two hours. Juliette found it hard, too, but at least it was a very good way of getting to know my new team-mates.

Bobby and Marco helped me enormously and took me under their wing while I adjusted to my new life in Ipswich. Without them, it would have been a much more lonely experience and I think it's fair to say they protected me a bit. It's probably thanks to them that I avoided any embarrassing

full english

In my comfort zone – I fitted in well and enjoyed getting to know my new Ipswich team-mates.

dressing room pranks or initiations. I hung out with them whenever possible and stayed at Bobby's house a few times (it gets a bit boring spending so much time in a hotel room). It was nice to chill out together in a more homely environment and watch a bit of TV, rather than being stuck within the same

"One memorable example is the food over here and I'll never forget coming down for breakfast on my first day, when I was presented with a Full English – a plate bulging with eggs, bacon, sausages, mushrooms, beans and toast."

four walls. I'll always be thankful to Bobby and his then girlfriend, Vanessa, and we stayed in touch during his time up at Celtic. Now, I'm afraid to say, we seem to have gone our separate ways but he was certainly a good mate at the time and the six of us – myself, Bobby, Marco and our other halves – had some lovely nights out in the restaurants of Ipswich.

I had a lot of spare time in the beginning, because we only trained once a day, with weight training thrown in before or after every session. Every now and again we did some running in the afternoon but not often. In England, we only trained twice a day for the first three months or so but in Holland we trained twice a day, on Tuesdays and Thursdays. It didn't matter if it was the beginning or the end of the season - it was always the same. In my spare time after training I stayed in the hotel and rested. Others would play games on their computer or go for a round of golf but that wasn't for me. I'm a lousy golfer anyway.

While it was nice to get out of the hotel, I've got nothing but fond memories for the staff there that helped make my transition so smooth. I made friends with some of them and they helped me adjust to the differences between life in Holland and England. One memorable example is the food over here and I'll never forget coming down for breakfast on my first day, when I was presented with a Full English – a plate bulging with eggs, bacon, sausages, mushrooms, beans and toast. I'd never seen anything like it in my life. I'm used to light breakfasts - cereal and then things like cheese or ham rolls. I just about managed my fry-up – something I've grown to love during my years here – but it was a bit of a struggle and hardly ideal energy food for my first training session.

I didn't want to seem rude or picky but had to say something afterwards and the staff – typically helpful – prepared something lighter and more suitable from then on. It's funny when I look back on my early days in this country because the first time I had that breakfast I thought it was disgusting and way too greasy. Now, I still think it's too greasy but really love beans on toast with a fried egg. My taste buds must have changed dramatically over the years.

I've always been very conscious about my diet. I see it as part and parcel of being a professional footballer. In Holland, people are more laid back and I saw football as nothing more than a hobby. Here it's a job and something to be professional about, which includes taking care of your fitness and diet. Issues like that become priorities and very much part of everyday life, which I've always enjoyed and taken seriously. I can't imagine it being any other way.

One other big difference between the countries, which I soon discovered, is the level of adulation players get here. As a professional back home, I could walk around as normal and even fans of my club would walk past, without even noticing me. People envy footballers and, as a result, can be a bit dismissive. Here, supporters look up to players and wherever you go – be it the supermarket, cinema or a restaurant – they want to stop and chat about the team and get an autograph. I love that. I enjoy meeting people and think it's great that they're so knowledgeable and enthusiastic. Again, I see it as part and parcel of my job and it's not something I've ever had a problem with.

It wasn't long before I had more company in the hotel in the shape of my new team-mate (and future boss) Jim Magilton. He initially arrived on loan from Sheffield Wednesday, before agreeing a £682,500 deal, and made his debut the week after me, in a televised 2-1 defeat at Sunderland. Again, I had massive problems understanding his broad Northern Irish accent but it was fantastic having him at the hotel and we got to know each other well. He was in the same boat as me because, for a short time at least, his family were still based up north. As everyone knows, Jim's a real character – lively, bubbly and loud. He's most definitely someone you hear before you see but a great and very natural leader. It came as no surprise to me that he later became club captain.

Unfortunately, something else we had in common was the fact both our debuts resulted in defeats. Jim's came in that top-of-the-table game at the Stadium of Light. Mine had been the previous weekend, at home to Grimsby. As with the early

full english

training sessions, there were a few butterflies fluttering inside me but, overall, I still felt surprisingly calm and confident – I knew I could do a job for this team. We lost 1-0 but I got the man-of-the-match bubbly, so it was a memorable day for me – if no one else.

After those back-to-back league defeats, we had a mouth-watering FA Cup third-round date up at Everton. We lost 1-0 (three losses in a row wasn't exactly what I'd had in mind) and, to make it even more sickening, I had what seemed a perfectly good goal ruled out. Richard Naylor was penalised for a push but I didn't realise and was off celebrating like a madman. Johno was practically hanging off my shoulder before the penny dropped and the sinking feeling set in. I can remember the Everton fans singing and laughing and giving me some stick, which got even worse later in the match.

There was another moment in that game which makes me shudder - albeit with a smile on my face - and I think it's the only time in my career I've been accused of being unsporting. Everton had kicked the ball out because one of their lads was injured. Adam Tanner took the throw and chucked it to me, expecting me to pass to one of their players or maybe back to the goalkeeper. Now, we've all seen that scenario a million times and it's considered the right and proper thing to do. However, I had no idea at the time. Adam shouted something as he threw the ball but I didn't understand. Burley also screamed at me from the dug out but, again, I didn't grasp it. There were only five minutes left and I thought they were saying keep it, keep it, keep it.

You have to understand that I'd only been in the country a couple of weeks and most of the time could barely understand a word from Burley or any of my team-mates. So instead of following protocol,

I ran with the ball – and ran and ran. Space opened up in front of me and suddenly I could see their goalkeeper. The opportunity was too good to miss so I had a shot and forced the keeper into a brilliant save.

For a second I was disappointed but, looking back, he did me a big favour – the whole thing would have been blown way out of proportion had I scored. The Everton fans were booing and jeering me, their players confronted me, pushing and swearing at me, and, for the rest of the evening, I was public enemy number one. Burley apologised on my behalf in his post-match press conference, explaining it was a simple mistake and that I didn't understand. Needless to say, it never happened again. I learnt the hard way and very much believe in being sporting – whatever the score or circumstances.

After playing three games and losing them all, the boys were joking that I was a bad omen and we'd dropped from second to fifth in the table. Thankfully, the losing trend was about to change. I want to avoid going into too much detail about game after game but, what I will say, is that win number one came in the next match at home to Port Vale and, from then on, with injured players returning and the new boys (Marlon Harewood, Jim and myself) gelling in, things were on the up. Including the Grimsby match, there were 20 league games left and I was fortunate enough to play in 18 of them (of which we won 12). I also scored my first goal for the club – another very important milestone moment – in a 6-0 romp at Swindon.

The two league games I missed were a 2-0 defeat at Bolton and a 1-0 home win against Stockport. I was out with a hamstring problem and, to be honest, was worried I might be out for longer.

I felt it go in training – the pain was unbearable - and it was such a setback, because I knew I was facing a spell on the sidelines. Any footballer will tell you that being injured is the worst thing possible, because you watch from the stands and you're powerless – apart from vocal encouragement you can't do anything to influence a game. It's horrible.

Thankfully, though, I've always been a quick healer and rather than being out for three weeks I was back in two and able to contribute again as a substitute in our next match, at home to Crewe (who fielded my future team-mates David Wright and Jermaine Wright). Those of you with a sharp memory will recall that we lost 2-1 – an outcome that undoubtedly acted as a hammer-blow to our promotion chances. It was an absolute sickener, coming three games from the end, and we only managed two wins in our final six matches – meaning we surrendered the second automatic promotion spot to Bradford. I can't begin to tell you how disappointing that was, especially having been in such a commanding position, and it meant the club were in the play-offs for the third year in a row.

For me, it was a new experience. I'd missed the league game up at Bolton a month before, so was more fired up than ever for the first leg at the Reebok. We lost 1-0 (the goal came six minutes from time) but it was still considered a decent result and it was most definitely a score we could overturn at Portman Road. Matty Holland put us in front – and therefore level – early in the second leg and the noise was unbelievable. It was deafening – as good as I ever heard during my time at the club – and at half-time Burley told us to stay positive and patient and keep doing the same things after the break. After that it developed into one of the most exciting games you'll ever see, even if it did finish in bitter disappointment and heartache.

We traded goals and eventually it needed a last-gasp header from Kieron to force extra-time, with the score 3-2 to us. It cancelled out our defeat three days earlier in the first leg but, although away goals didn't count at the end of 90 minutes, we knew they would do after extra-time. Everyone was buzzing because we suddenly had the momentum but, from my point of view, I was absolutely and totally exhausted – dead and buried. I'd given everything and just couldn't run anymore. I just about managed 15 more minutes before having to be replaced by Micky Stockwell.

To then lose on away goals was shattering. As you can imagine, the dressing room was like a morgue. No one said anything – what could you say? - because the lads had got so close and given their all, only to have the dream ripped away in the cruellest of fashions. The vast majority of the players – myself included, obviously – hadn't sampled Premier League football and in that situation you question whether you'll get another opportunity. We were very, very down and gauging the mood of the supporters – and of the town and area in general – really brought it home to me how important the club is to so many people. We felt we'd let them down. We didn't even give them a day out at Wembley. The lads went their separate ways for the summer and were forced to dwell and reflect on what had happened. It was like a recurring nightmare but, if there was a positive to be gleaned, it made us even more determined to put things right the following season.

full english

the only way is up

Like the other boys, I was definitely up for the challenge ahead. However, I have to hold my hands up and admit I was both naïve and unprofessional during the summer of 1999. In fact, the close season was nothing short of a personal disaster. It was my first with the club but, I'm ashamed to say, I didn't take it anywhere near as seriously as I should have done. With it also being my first English summer, I had so many family members and friends queuing up to come and visit from Holland. I was the proud host, more than happy to show off my new surroundings and together we'd have days out and see the sights – places like Colchester, Felixstowe and London.

While that may not seem like a problem, it meant I wasn't doing what I should be doing – relaxing and recharging my batteries for the rigours of a new season. Just the opposite, in fact. The whole cycle of people coming to see us, staying and then going home again – coupled with all the days and nights out – really took its toll and I was shattered, a total spent force. The club had given us a strict exercise regime to follow in the weeks between the end of the season and recommencing for training. It started with two weeks of complete rest, after the second play-off match against Bolton. Then we were allowed to do things like golf, tennis and swimming before finally, a fortnight before we reconvened, we could start jogging. I have to admit, I didn't follow it at all. I didn't do anything and how that came back to haunt me when we got back together to start training.

> "Arrogantly, I thought I could get away without putting in the work and was confident I'd still be OK. I thought it would be a walk in the park. How wrong can you be."

Pre-season is very different in Holland. There, the emphasis is on a slow, patient build-up. Here, it is the complete opposite and we were pushed to the limit from day one. We were doing all different running distances and I didn't know what had hit me. The idea is that players are super-fit right from the start but I struggled terribly. I was just so tired and very aware that I was behind the other lads, which in itself was a dreadful, sinking feeling. After so many pre-seasons since I've come to know what to expect, but then I didn't have a clue and was caught out big time.

One day during training we had a running test, whereby we had to race a certain distance (I forget how far) inside six minutes. Needless to say, I didn't make it and my punishment was being ordered in for an extra training session the following Saturday. To add to my humiliation, I was the only player who didn't pass so was there on my own. It was just me and George Burley and he made me run and run around the grounds of Ufford Park. Fair play to the boss. He was livid that I was so under prepared and I had no one to blame but myself – my fitness was rubbish and I'd let myself down.

I wasn't close to being fit and, looking back, feel I learnt the hard way. It was without doubt the hardest, most gruelling and harrowing pre-season of my entire career. No footballer really likes that time of year. It can become a bit boring and repetitive and in many ways you're going through the motions, trying to build up a basic level of fitness which is then fundamental to everything you do. For me, though, that one was far worse – it was a nightmare. Arrogantly, I thought I could get away without putting in the work and was confident I'd still be OK. I thought it would be a walk in the park. How wrong can you be. I can see all this now, with the benefit of time and experience on my side.

The whole fitness issue had an effect on my home life, too, because I'd get home and go straight to bed. I'd literally lay there shaking because I was so physically and mentally exhausted. I felt sick and dreaded going in for training. The importance of pre-season has been instilled in me ever since and, if I ever coach or manage a team, it's something I'll always be acutely aware of.

Quite rightly (I didn't think it at the time but can see it now), Burley punished me by putting me on the bench for the first couple of games. I got a start at Swindon, then found myself back among the substitutes for our game against Bolton. There were so many matches in a short space of time and I just couldn't cope. Back then, though, I didn't have the maturity to understand why the manager wasn't playing me – I blamed him and thought he was against me, that there was something personal between us. I was annoyed with him and he was

cross with me and, with the benefit of hindsight, I can safely say that was the beginning of the end, in terms of our relationship.

Team-wise, we made a decent start to the new campaign, enjoyed a six-game unbeaten run and were the early leaders of Division One. We also managed 17 goals (conceding just six) and put three past Nottingham Forest, four past Swindon and a whopping six past Barnsley. Our new signings, John McGreal and Jermaine Wright, settled in nicely and I got on well with them both. John's a great guy – impossible not to become friends with – and the same goes for Jamma, who first turned up while we were away on our pre-season tour. I think his trip must have been hastily arranged, because he hardly had any clothes with him. On his first night, we decided to go out as a group and have a drink together – and he had to borrow my jeans and shirt. It was a strange sight because we'd barely had a chance to speak up to that point, yet here I was having a conversation with my new team-mate wearing my clothes.

On the flip side, Bobby Petta moved on to Celtic. That was obviously a real blow for me personally and I was sad to see him go, but knew it was an excellent opportunity and wouldn't have wanted to see him miss out. Kieron Dyer also moved on in a £6 million transfer to Newcastle. As with Bobby, it was a real setback to lose one of our best players but I could fully understand his reasons. It was too good a chance to turn down.

Our first defeat came in a home game against Birmingham and then, in the days before our next match, we welcomed a new player to the ranks – Gary Croft – who managed a goal on his debut against Manchester City. What a character he was. I got on famously with him and we stayed in touch

after he moved on. In fact, I was invited to his wedding last summer but unfortunately couldn't make it because we were away on holiday. When fans think of Crofty, I'm sure they all think of the same incident – his infamous brush with the law (for driving while disqualified and attempting to pervert the course of justice). He made history as the first professional footballer to wear an electronic tag during games (a whole new concept to me). I'd never be so stupid as to condone what he did. It was daft and irresponsible and he knows that better than anyone. However, I can vouch for my old team-mate and safely say he hasn't got a malicious bone in his body. He's a joker who likes a prank, but he never set out to hurt anyone. He just didn't think about the consequences of his actions.

I was driving to training with him, David Johnson and one other player I can't for the life of me remember when Crofty was first arrested. We were in his car and literally just a few minutes from the training ground in Bent Lane. Suddenly, we saw a police car parked in the road ahead and I remember Crofty making a shocked, worried remark. The rest of us didn't have the slightest clue what was going on and it stayed that way for the next few minutes. The police made us stop and, speaking to our driver, asked 'are you Mr Croft?' When Crofty gave them the answer they were looking for, he was asked to get out and into the back of their car.

We just sat there watching and listening with our jaws wide open. We didn't have any inkling what the problem was and started whispering and speculating. Then one of the policemen asked if myself, Johno or the other player (who was it?!) could drive Crofty's car to the training ground. "We have to take Mr Croft to the police station to answer some questions," continued the policeman. Johno did the honours and drove us for the remaining couple of minutes to Bent Lane. He was also quick to report the problem to Burley, too, who went off to get more information.

Dale Roberts took training that morning and, at the end, Burley called us all together for a team meeting. When he told us what had happened, we were gobsmacked. Crofty was forced to miss our next match at Grimsby and then, in the ensuing weeks, served about a month of his four-month prison sentence. Upon his release, he then had to wear the tag for our home match against Swindon in the January. Everyone was taking the mickey out of him but he took it in good heart. As I said, he did a bad thing but we all make mistakes. It doesn't alter the fact he's a very nice, outgoing and bubbly guy – a great friend and team-mate during our time together at Town.

Football-wise, things were going well. We enjoyed an 18-game unbeaten run, spanning early November to the start of March, and during that time we felt we could win every game. We had so much momentum and belief and, to this day, it never ceases to amaze me what a difference confidence makes within a dressing room. In many ways it's the most important thing. Even if we weren't playing well we knew we were capable of nicking or grinding out a win. We'd stand there in the tunnel and eye up our opposition, smugly thinking to ourselves 'they've got no chance'. That's how bullish we were at the time – we felt invincible. Unfortunately, that wasn't the case, as we were soon to discover.

During that run of games, Burley decided to splash some cash and bolster our attacking options by signing Marcus Stewart, from fellow play-off chasers Huddersfield. He made a positive impact, chipping in goals on his debut at Barnsley and then the following week against (ironically) Huddersfield. Unfortunately, injuries and a loss of form meant he failed to score again until the play-off final, but he was still a very important and valued member of our squad for the run-in.

In many ways, Stewy's problem mirrored that of the team for a while. After flying high and enjoying that wonderful run, we only managed two points from five games – a sequence that put a huge spanner in the works of our promotion dream. And, to make matters worse, that sequence finished with a 2-0 defeat at home to the old enemy, Norwich. I still wince when I remember that game as I know I didn't play well. Worse still, I misjudged a high ball which allowed Iwan Roberts to score one of their goals. During a spell like that, the opposite applies in terms of mental approach. Far from feeling invincible, you think 'here we go again'. Every bad refereeing decision, bounce, break or deflection seems to conspire against you and it's horrible, because you're stuck in a rut. As I said, confidence is everything in football – I firmly believe that.

It was time for another fresh face and next to arrive was a player destined to become my very good friend, Martijn Reuser. A winning goal on his debut at Fulham gave us a real lift and he helped us pocket 15 points from our last six games – only to be pipped to the second promotion spot by Manchester City. As I said earlier, Martijn was a bit mouthy and arrogant to start with – in my opinion, typical of someone from Amsterdam! He had a different, very sarcastic sense of humour which people over here weren't used to. They didn't understand some of the things he said and when they did they got offended, but I thought he was hilarious and from day one we clicked. I suppose I looked after him in those early days like Bobby and Marco did for me and we became great friends (and soon room-mates).

Looking back, we went through so much together during our time at the club – joy and despair – and we were best mates, spending a lot of time together away from the club. We also had some evenings out together when I introduced him to the local night scene. I don't mean this in a disrespectful way and I love Ipswich, but for two city boys (me from Rotterdam and him from Amsterdam) it wasn't exactly wild. Martijn kept thinking there was more to see and I think initially he was a bit disappointed, but we still had great fun together and he soon came to love the town and area as much as me.

full english

Martijn was a big part of our success late in the season. We finished strongly but, once again, found ourselves entering the total lottery of the play-offs (for the fourth year in a row). Again, our opposition were Bolton. To be honest, I don't remember much about the first game, apart from wildly celebrating in front of the Town fans when Marcus hauled us back to 2-2, after being two-down and minus the injured Johno and Tony Mowbray. For the second game, I was an unused substitute, which was bitterly disappointing. It was one of those big games and occasions everyone wants to be part of, so to be on the bench – and stay there for the whole match – was unbearable, especially as I'd contributed in 35 of the league games.

The night itself was extraordinary, a real roller coaster ride of drama and emotion. Bolton, to be fair, played some excellent, offensive football, which I suppose they had to because of the away goals we'd managed at the Reebok. To add to the drama, they also had two men sent off. Jim was outstanding that night. The pace and tempo of the game was amazing and we eventually triumphed 5-3, thanks to extra-time goals by Jamie Clapham and Martijn after Jim had claimed his first senior hat-trick. He was like a man possessed and, I'm sure, the fittest player on the pitch. He kept going and going and you could practically see the adrenaline pulsing through his body.

In terms of other special memories of the night, Martijn's goal was the one that clinched it and killed them off. It was only then that the unbearable tension was finally over, because we knew the game was won. Bolton didn't have the energy levels to come back. Our super-sub had done it again, although I can tell you he absolutely hated that tag. Time and again he'd step off the bench and make a difference, but he was always moaning about being called a super-sub. To him it was a bit of an insult, because he was so desperate to start and felt he was good enough to be in the team every week. At one stage he was actually very down about his lack of chances. I used to bear the brunt of his complaints and would tell him that at least he stood a decent chance of coming on. If the team were losing he'd play and even when we were winning the manager might decide to freshen up his attacking options. He was what you'd call an impact player.

For me, as a defender, I felt there was a good chance that if I started on the bench I'd stay there and that, unfortunately, was the way it panned out in the second leg against Bolton. Even though I didn't play, that game was one of the most exciting of my whole career. The pace and drama was like nothing I'd experienced before and, to this day, I still think there's something special about a big game under the Portman Road floodlights. I was so disappointed not to have played but thrilled at the prospect of going to Wembley. We had the chance to etch our names in the history books as it was the last domestic match at the old stadium, so, if ever there was a time to do it, it was now.

We were also acutely aware of what our achievement meant to so many people. We'd made a lot of supporters very, very happy and that was a proud and special feeling. Now we had the chance to change their lives and also our own. The challenge was there to jump the last hurdle, beat Barnsley in the play-off final and book our spot among the elite of English football.

living the dream

After such a long and heady celebration following our Wembley heroics, the thrilling reality kicked in – we were Premier League footballers. It was hard to digest at first and incredible to think that we, little Ipswich Town, were about to rub shoulders with the giants of the English game – the big, household names and all the heavyweight teams like Liverpool, Chelsea, Arsenal and Manchester United. Given the enormity of the task, it was no surprise our preparations were different that summer. It was such a hard, gruelling pre-season – one of the toughest I ever encountered during my career. The focus was different and everything we did was for a much bigger reason and specific purpose.

W e knew we weren't going to be the best footballers in the division so the theory was that we'd compensate in other ways, by being extremely fit. We might not be able to outplay teams in a football sense but hoped we might out-run them.

We had to adjust to becoming Premier League players, in terms of our eating and sleeping habits, and

Sticking to his principles – George Burley was adamant we should retain our passing philosophy in the Premier League.

get used to so much more exposure – both on the club and as individuals. Camera crews from all over the world came to watch us train and life changed for everyone. Whereas before I'd only get recognised in and around Ipswich, suddenly people would approach me when I walked down a road in London. There was media interest in me back home in Holland, too, and even suggestions that I might be on the verge of a call-up to the national team (something that sadly didn't materialize, mainly due to the stiff competition from Michael Reiziger at Barcelona).

Burley was determined that every one of his players would be super fit and, to his credit, he was also adamant that we should maintain our footballing principles. He wanted us to keep the ball down and be regarded as a decent, passing side – a philosophy that certainly met with the players' approval. Everyone felt very comfortable on the ball and it was our eye-catching approach that had guided us to promotion in the first place. There was no need to abandon that policy just because we were in the Premier League.

Despite it being such a happy and upbeat time, I have to say that my summer had been marred by a major fall-out with Burley. We had a disagreement over our forthcoming tour of Latvia, Finland and

Estonia. Juliette will explain it in her chapter but, to cut a long story short, it concerned me having to go on tour – despite the fact she had just given birth to Jada. I had no option but to join up with the rest of the lads for one (in my eyes) meaningless friendly. When I arrived at the team's hotel, the lads couldn't believe it. They weren't expecting me and were amazed when I told them what had happened. To say I didn't do myself justice in the match would be an understatement. I had to play the full 90 minutes and that, for the first time in my career, felt like torture. My only sleep had been on the flight to Latvia. I was so tired, having been up all night with the baby. The whole thing had been a total waste of time.

What was the point in me being out there when my wife and newborn baby were at home? I was only there just over a day when I had to turn round and come back again. In any other walk of life I would have been given paternity leave, yet that privilege had been taken away from me and I'll never understand why. It was a very frustrating time but, despite the issues between the manager and myself, I was absolutely determined to prove him wrong. A lesser player might have given in but I tried to keep going and believing. And as the season progressed, I like to think I didn't give him many opportunities to fault me or, better still, drop me.

After our lung-busting summer, training two or three times a day, the big-kick off came at Tottenham. It was an unbelievable venue to start at and a ground that simply breathed history and tradition. The major disappointment from my point of view, once again, was that I started on the bench. It was deja vu after what happened at Wembley, but Burley wanted to keep faith with the players that had performed such heroics to get us up. Mark Venus lashed us in front with a free-kick – I think I'm right in saying it was the first goal of the Premier League season – but Spurs, inspired by their new £11 million Ukrainian Sergei Rebrov, proved too strong and won 3-1.

So we made a disappointing start, but there was no time to dwell on it because just three days later we had our first home game against none other than Manchester United. What an occasion that was and not least for me, just a day before my 30th birthday. It was the game I'd waited my entire career for and the day before, on the Monday, I got the news I'd been so desperate to receive – I was in from the start in place of Gary Croft. That night I laid awake in bed for ages, imagining the game in my head. I was nervous – who wouldn't be? – and it was quite an introduction as I'd be in direct competition with their wing wizard, Ryan Giggs. Welcome to the Premier League. I still had confidence in myself, though, and was determined to enjoy the occasion.

For so many reasons, the big night itself was to prove truly unforgettable. The noise level inside the ground was unbelievable - certainly the best I ever experienced. United were fresh from winning the treble the previous season and their team was packed with legends like Giggs, David Beckham, Roy Keane and Andy Cole. It was a classic case of David v Goliath. Despite that, though, we – and me in particular – enjoyed an explosive start. Defensively, I'd hoped and prayed

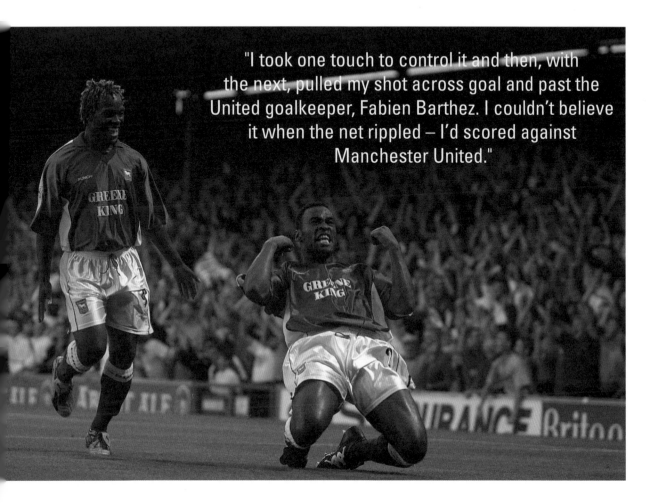

"I took one touch to control it and then, with the next, pulled my shot across goal and past the United goalkeeper, Fabien Barthez. I couldn't believe it when the net rippled – I'd scored against Manchester United."

to do myself justice but to score a goal was beyond my wildest dreams. It was pure fantasy and I'll never forget the build-up.

Pure instinct kicked in when their full-back moved inside – leaving an ocean of space in front of me. I couldn't believe it and just ran and ran, from inside my own half and away from their nearest player, Giggs. Thankfully, David Johnson noticed and played the most perfect ball into my path. I took one touch to control it and then, with the next, pulled my shot across goal and past the United goalkeeper, Fabien Barthez. I couldn't believe it when the net rippled – I'd scored against Manchester United. As a defender, I never expected to score many goals but to get one against them was just unreal and I didn't know what to do with myself. The wall of noise was extraordinary and my ecstatic facial expressions – captured so vividly in the next day's newspapers - said it all.

full english

It was so special, not just for me but for my family, too. Juliette couldn't be there as Jada was only a month old and we didn't feel ready to leave her but my brother, Kenneth, had travelled over from Holland. Apparently he went absolutely mad after the goal, telling everyone around him that I was his brother.

The only thing that would have capped my night would have been if we'd managed to hang on for three points. Beckham whipped in a free-kick to equalise but even after that we had chances to win. Afterwards, Sir Alex Ferguson was very complimentary – about our crowd and our performance. He said we'd do fine in the division and, coming from him, that meant a lot. I had to do interviews with the BBC and Sky and in both of them I said my goal was a 'dream come true'. The amount of stick I got from the lads afterwards was amazing. Jim made the most of it for a couple of months and every time he saw me at the start of training he'd say the prophetic words about me 'having a dream', after the world-famous speech by Martin Luther King.

The day after the game my delirious face graced the front page of the Evening Star, alongside the headline Fabulous Fab, and they very kindly gave me a framed copy, which I still treasure. Of course, it was also my 30th birthday and I spent it celebrating with Juliette, my two girls, Martijn Reuser and his girlfriend, Petra. I couldn't believe my eyes when I opened my present from Juliette. It was a copy of Sir Alex Ferguson's autobiography and Juliette had somehow managed to get it signed. The events of the previous night were still going round and round in my mind and I couldn't stop looking at the words 'To Fabian, Happy Birthday, Sir Alex Ferguson'. Perfect.

At the start of the season we'd seen a sports psychologist and one of the main things he discussed was our hopes and expectations for the season. He asked us all to think how many points we realistically expected to have after our first three Premier League games. Burley said six or seven. I thought four would represent a solid start. We'd only got one from the first two games but soon we were up to four, after Titus Bramble powered us to a 1-0 home victory against Sunderland. I think the whole team was hanging off him as he celebrated in front of the North Stand. Our decent start had got us thinking. It was still very early days but there was already a feeling that we could hold our own in the division. It was all about getting to 40 points – the usual safety mark – as soon as possible and that was our priority.

That defiance was dented a little after the next game, a 2-1 defeat against Aston Villa, but most people there that day – myself included – may remember it more for the terrible, career-ending injury suffered by Luc Nilis. I knew it was serious straight away and must admit it shakes you up to see a fellow player in such distress. I didn't know Luc personally but had played against him many times in Holland. He'd been a top goal scorer back home and once had a brilliant partnership with Ruud van Nistelrooy at PSV Eindhoven. I saw the photos of his collision with Richard Wright in the papers the following day and it made me feel sick. Such a promising career had been wiped out in a second and people in this country never saw the best of him. It certainly gets you thinking. I feel so fortunate to have got through my entire career without a serious, long-term injury. I've been lucky, but I also like to think I've looked after myself and done as much as possible to prolong my career. I've

"I asked Thierry Henry to swap shirts but Titus had already beaten me to it. Then I asked Bergkamp but, again, one of the other boys had got there first."

full english

always enjoyed yoga and had regular massages to keep myself flexible and without things like that I'd never have played so long.

Hero of the hour – James Scowcroft joins in the celebrations after my dramatic winning goal at Coventry City.

The man with the goal-den touch - Marcus Stewart performed heroics during our wonderful first season back in the Premier League. He scored 19 goals, including a famous winner against Liverpool at Anfield.

The other significant thing about the Villa game was that Marcus Stewart was on the score sheet – the first in a magical season that saw him finish with an incredible 19 Premier League goals. He was such a pivotal figure in our team that year, mainly for the goals but also for the confidence he instilled in the rest of us. Everything he touched turned to gold and it was encouraging for the rest of us to know that if he got one chance, more often than not he'd bury it. Sometimes you wouldn't notice him in the game for 85 minutes but he'd still emerge as our match winner. If we could just create openings for him, we had a decent chance in every game – regardless of the opposition.

We were fortunate to have a brilliant, solid defence at that time. We had the very talented Richard Wright in goal, the energetic Hermann Hreidarsson as left-back, me on the right and the centre-backs were between Titus Bramble, John McGreal and Mark Venus. We kept 13 clean sheets and only conceded 15 goals at Portman Road (42 in total). That's a remarkably low amount considering it was our very first year back in the top flight, with players who hadn't experienced a single minute at that level before.

After a brilliant win at Leeds, our next Premier League match was against mighty Arsenal at Portman Road. Stewy put us in front just after the break and only a very late equaliser from Dennis Bergkamp salvaged a point for the Gunners. It was still an impressive result against top-class opposition, though, and the only disappointment was that I didn't get a memento from the big game. I asked Thierry Henry to swap shirts but Titus had already beaten me to it. Then I asked Bergkamp but, again, one of the other boys had got there first (I can't remember who!) I wanted to give up after that but had one more go and asked Martin Keown. He willingly gave his shirt to me and I still treasure it, along with the many others I collected that season.

Our season was building momentum and, after our next win, a surprisingly easy 3-0 victory at Everton, the boys were buzzing. Again, Marcus had an unbelievable game and the lads were singing and dancing during the long journey home. We were going from strength to strength and the fact we'd beaten quality opposition so convincingly gave us the feeling we might be on the verge of something special. We hadn't been outplayed by anyone so far and maybe, just maybe, we could set our sights a bit higher than just survival. We'd embarked on a winning run and, although there were occasional blips in the coming weeks, confidence within the squad remained sky high. There was tremendous unity in the camp and a key reason was the fact we knew each other so well. Hermann had been our only addition during the summer so, generally speaking, it was the same bunch of lads that got us promoted the season before.

Burley had kept faith with the players that served him so well – perhaps he should have stuck to that philosophy the following season (more of which later) – and, as a group of players, we got on famously. That's not me wearing rose-tinted glasses – we really were that close and religiously made a point of going out together once a month, sometimes for a quiet drink or sometimes to big parties (I've got great memories of some fancy dress dos). We enjoyed each other's company and saw each other as friends, rather than just colleagues.

The points kept rolling in and only some bloke called Shearer denied us maximum points up at Newcastle. Even then they needed a controversial penalty to get the better of us. Among the successes, of course, was our famous victory at Liverpool.

What a day that was and what a venue Anfield is – the embodiment of everything special about British football. I'd grown up as a Liverpool fan, when the likes of John Barnes and Ian Rush were the kings not only of England but also of Europe. The atmosphere was unbelievable that day and, for me, nowhere else comes close. Emerging from the tunnel – having watched every Liverpool player reach up and touch the 'Welcome to Anfield' sign - into that wall of noise and passion was actually quite intimidating. I had goose bumps all over my body, not least after the almighty roar that followed You'll Never Walk Alone.

Nerve-racking it might have been but it was also very inspiring. It gave the boys a massive boost and we were desperate to show those fans how good we could be. Once again, we were indebted to Stewy. He scored the only goal of the game – an incredible, unexpected winner – to stun the Kop and what a cool, composed finish it was. He almost passed the ball into the net.

Liverpool threw absolutely everything at us after that. They kept pumping the ball forward and keeping a clean sheet in those circumstances, against strikers of the calibre of Robbie Fowler and Michael Owen, was an immense achievement. To hold on and take three points from Liverpool gave our soaring confidence another huge lift. In fact, I'd go so far as to say that a feeling of arrogance crept in. People may deem that a negative but I saw it as a positive, because we were going into games expecting to win. If someone had said that to me in the summer, I'd have laughed.

full english

The next big highlight for me was our match against Coventry City at Highfield Road. No one else probably remembers much about it and I can understand why, because it was a horrible, scrappy match – a real bore for the audience watching on Sky. The game was also being shown live back home in Holland. For 90 minutes, it had been so dull. Then, in a flash, I played the ball out wide to Martijn and kept on running, right into the Coventry box. He whipped over a cross and I managed a diving header to plant the ball firmly in the back of the net. I'd done it again. What a feeling that was – there can't be many better experiences in football than scoring a last-gasp winner like that. Again, my friends at the Evening Star gave me a framed back page to commemorate my achievements.

From feeling invincible, we were to get a bit of a reality check just before Christmas in the 2-0 defeat at Manchester United. For me, it was my first ever visit to Old Trafford. It was absolutely fantastic, but I did feel a bit over-whelmed by the size of the ground. To think of all the huge games United had played there in the league and Europe. It was a bit unreal to be there now. It was the first game in which we had no chances and were well and truly outplayed. We were over-awed, didn't get our usual passing game together and, to be perfectly honest, never had a kick. It was particularly disappointing as Juliette was there in the crowd and so was my good friend Olaf Lindebergh (the former Ajax player).

It was certainly a kick in the teeth but, thankfully, we soon overcame the disappointment. More points followed during a typically gruelling festive period (four games in eight days) and the other big winter bonus was our continued success in the League Cup. We got to the semi-finals, where we met Birmingham City, but missed so many chances in the first leg at Portman Road. We won 1-0, but to this day I've got no idea how we didn't score more goals. It was a failure which came back to haunt us and, for me personally, it was a particularly disappointing day.

We always travelled to away matches the day before to get the best possible preparation. However, instead of doing something light like going for a walk, we trained so hard on the morning of the second leg that I pulled a hamstring. It annoys me just thinking about it because I don't understand why we were pushed so much. Fitness was never an issue as we'd just played all those games over Christmas. It seemed an unnecessary exertion and, because of my injury, I had to miss out and watch the game from the dugout next to Titus. We lost 4-1 and missing out on a return trip to Wembley, having got within one game, was heartbreaking.

My injury kept me out for three games in total and we lost them all (against Birmingham, Leeds and Arsenal) so I like to think the boys missed me. I managed to get my place back and there were more highs as our unbelievable season reached its latter stages. To eventually finish fifth, and be in with a shout of Champions League football on the final day, was pure fantasy and no one would have thought it possible back in August. People often ask me what the secret was and, for me, the over riding factor was the team spirit I mentioned. We really clicked, worked tirelessly for each other and knew each other's strengths and weaknesses – using them to full potential.

To have played in the vast majority of the games, against all the big stars and household names, makes me eternally proud and grateful. I never thought I'd get the chance to face legends like Bergkamp, Henry, Beckham and Giggs and,

Proud man – I was so happy and grateful to have played
such a big part in our historic Premier League season.

for giving me that opportunity, I've got nothing but praise and respect for my team-mates. There was a real cocktail of personalities in the dressing room and everyone gelled well. We were fortunate to have an inspirational skipper in Matty Holland. He was a top-class professional, a great ambassador for the club and a thoroughly nice guy – every bit as pleasant and genuine as his public image. He was a great servant to the club and how he played all those consecutive games I'll never know. Sometimes we called him Matty Friday, because due to injury he wouldn't train all week apart from Friday. Then, somehow, after being a doubt, he'd recover in the nick of time.

There were the loud ones in the dressing room, like Veno. What an articulate, witty and quick-thinking guy he was – great fun and a certainty to go into the management side of things. Jim and Marcus also definitely fell into that category and so too did my good friend Hermann. In fact, he was more than loud – he was a nutter. He lived in the same road as us so we spent a lot of time together and I loved him to bits, because he was so honest and true to himself. Once Juliette and myself went with him on a little holiday to his native Iceland. They don't have many big celebrities out there and he and his wife, Ragna, are like the Posh and Becks, because she played for and coached the Icelandic female team. I hit it off with him straight away and it makes me smile thinking about some of his madcap antics around the training ground.

Martijn was my other great buddy at that time. I knew of him and what kind of player he was from his early days in Holland, but we hadn't actually met until he joined Ipswich. To start with Martijn rubbed a few people up the wrong way. He was so sarcastic and it definitely annoyed people at times,

full english

Getting stuck in – here I am in the thick of the action during our home match with Aston Villa.

even me and I was his friend! We became really close, though, and he definitely matured during his time at the club, especially after becoming a dad for the first time. He became a lot more responsible, although that cheeky streak was never too far away. One story comes to mind and that was when we played up at Sunderland on New Year's Day. As usual, we were rooming together and both of us were a bit flat the evening before the game because we were away from our loved ones on such a special night. New Year's Eve is a big deal in Holland – bigger than here – and we decided we fancied a little drink to toast our families. We weren't planning anything wild, just a glass of wine to see in 2001. The mini bar in our room was empty (on the manager's orders) so we called room service to get a bottle of red sent up. "Are you the footballers?" came a stern, disapproving voice on the other end of the line. When we replied that we were, we were told that Burley had given hotel staff specific instructions not to give any of us alcohol.

Surely one little glass wouldn't do us any harm, we thought. Thwarted but defiant, we went out into the corridor and found a room maid. We offered her £20 to go and buy us a bottle but, true to her orders, she turned us down. By now we were more determined than ever so went down to the hotel lobby, sneaked into a private party in one of the function rooms and finally, at last, got our hands on a bottle of red. Looking back, that was probably the highlight of that particular New Year. We couldn't get through to our loved ones, because the phone lines were so busy, and then the next day we lost 4-1 at the Stadium of Light. Hardly the best start to 2001.

Thankfully, the highs very much outweighed the lows and finishing fifth was a monumental achievement, not to mention the fact we qualified for the UEFA Cup. There were two main reasons – we'd worked extremely hard and also, as I keep mentioning, the spirit and unity in the camp. It can't be under estimated and, in terms of banter, it was unbelievable and the best I ever experienced. However, it was an injection of new faces and personalities which rocked the ship the following summer. And it was that change of mood in the dressing room which undoubtedly contributed to our struggles and eventual relegation.

a clash of cultures

Having worked so tirelessly to get up, then finish fifth, it was always going to be difficult to emulate our success of 2000-01. To be so high in the table and qualify for Europe again was an unbelievable achievement and a huge milestone in the history of Ipswich Town. However, it meant expectations were sky-high for the following season – from the supporters as well as us, the players – and that undoubtedly hung like a noose round our neck as the campaign unfolded.

On a personal note, I felt prepared. Off my own back and eager to learn from my previous mistakes, I returned a week before most of the other players to make sure I was in tip-top condition and to do some extra work with our fitness coach, Simon Thadani. I always found it much easier preparing and working around other people, rather than motivating myself to go for a run round the park or to the gym on my own. Simon was excellent, too, and a real fountain of knowledge to the players – always more than happy to help and pass on his expertise. After the horror of my first pre-season at the club, I swore that would never, ever happen again and now here I was in prime condition ready for the challenge of what promised to be another exciting season. Generally, hopes were understandably high and I wanted to be a major part of whatever lay ahead, just as I had been in our previous successful season in the Premier League.

> "Understandably, Andy's nose was put well and truly out of joint by Matteo's arrival and it's certainly fair to say the two of them never saw eye to eye."

Off the pitch, as most people are aware, it was a strange summer as a wind of change swept through Portman Road. For me, the whole feel of the club became different as new, big name and big money signings arrived. The main two that spring to mind are Matteo Sereni and Finidi George. Matteo joined on the eve of the season in a club record £5 million move from Sampdoria. He came with a reputation and the personality and character to match it. To me, he always looked like a movie star – incredibly well groomed, nicely tanned, very stylish and very Italian – extremely different to some of the other lads in the dressing room who took a disliking to him straight away.

They thought he was arrogant but I felt differently. In fact, I was one of the few who liked him and clicked with him right from the off. He rolled up at the club looking typically immaculate and, as someone with a passion for clothes and fashion, I was impressed. To me,

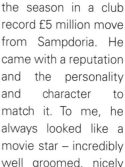

Big name, big reputation – Matteo Sereni.

One-hit wonder? – Finidi George.

Are you OK? - Matteo stands over me in the goal-mouth after I picked up an injury.

he was very cool and even a bit of an inspiration. I tend to judge people as I find them and he certainly never did anything to annoy or upset me, so I was happy to be his friend.

For someone who barely spoke a word of English, Matteo was also very loud and vocal – traits which probably didn't endear him to some people. To me, he was just lively and funny, though, and we got on well, despite the language barrier. He taught me some Italian – no doubt swear words - and I loved the way he was so emotional and expressive in the way he spoke. Sometimes I'd see him around the training ground, speaking on his mobile phone and think he was embroiled in an argument with someone. He'd talk at the top of his voice and wave his arms around – body language which, to me, suggests confrontation. Then he'd coolly come off the phone and say it was just a routine call to his wife or mum. Matteo would be the first to admit it took him time to adjust to life in England. He was under pressure because of the bumper price tag hanging round his neck and he needed a while to settle before he could start living up to his reputation.

His arrival had been a big surprise because earlier in the summer the club had snapped up Andy Marshall on a free transfer from Norwich. Andy had been seen as our new number one and an ideal replacement for Arsenal-bound Richard Wright. Unfortunately, though, he suffered a back injury, which was initially thought to be quite serious. That led to the hunt for a replacement and now, almost on the eve of the new campaign, the club had splashed out on a new, expensive goalkeeper. Understandably, Andy's nose was put well and truly out of joint by Matteo's arrival and it's certainly fair to say the two of them never saw eye to eye. Goalkeepers usually room together for away games but there would have been a few fireworks if that had happened with those two.

Andy was such a nice guy and I felt sorry for him, partly because of Matteo and partly because he was on a hiding to nothing at Ipswich. Given his former club and the rivalry, he was given a rough ride from day one and, I have to say, some of our fans were unfair to him. I'm sure

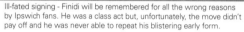

Ill-fated signing - Finidi will be remembered for all the wrong reasons by Ipswich fans. He was a class act but, unfortunately, the move didn't pay off and he was never able to repeat his blistering early form.

Down but not out – Martijn Reuser hooks his boot round the ball during our home match with Derby.

it was only a minority but I don't see how any supporter can justify booing and taunting one of their own players. Andy got stick when he played well and slaughtered when he made a mistake, so couldn't do anything right.

Finidi was the other big arrival during the summer of 2001, costing in excess of £3 million from Real Mallorca. I actually knew him reasonably well from our respective time in Holland (as a player, rather than personally). In fact, I played against him lots of times when I was with Breda and he was at Ajax. As he was a right-winger and I was a left full-back at the time, our paths crossed on many occasions. Finidi was very experienced and, in his prime, skilful and quick. He was some player and, to be honest, I was very surprised when George Burley managed to lure him to Ipswich. It was great news, though, because I knew he was quality. I could speak to him without any problems as his Dutch was good and Finidi already had one ally at the club as he knew Martijn, from their time together at Ajax. In fact, he conferred with his old pal before signing on the dotted line. Finidi was a really nice guy – gentle, quiet and very much a person who kept himself to himself. He was never one of the lads, in terms of socialising.

Mention the name Finidi George to any Town fan and they'll all remember the same game – our home match with Derby in August 2001. I came off the bench in that match, as

Double Dutch – Martijn became one of my best friends.

my frustrating start to the season continued, but the night well and truly belonged to our new Nigerian. He scored two goals and produced an unbelievable performance – one of the best ever by a right-winger, according to Burley. Who could forget his goal celebrations, either? He ran to the fans and planted a huge kiss on one ecstatic supporter's face, then grabbed a hat from someone and did a little dance. How he enjoyed his moment in the spotlight, but how disappointing he was never able to repeat that explosive form. In many ways, he was a one-hit wonder.

Another signing around that time, which I found odd, was Ulrich Le Pen. Not because of money, reputation or personality but because he was the tiniest player I've ever come across. He was so thin, lacked any kind of bulk or muscle and just didn't look like a professional footballer. It makes me smile when I think about it because when he made his debut he was wearing a shirt two or three times too big – he looked more like our mascot than our new signing. Burley really pushed him in training and the lad didn't know what had hit him. He just couldn't cope. Poor Ulrich was very skilful but just not strong enough, especially for the Premier League. He only played a handful of minutes for the club but when he did he got knocked off the ball so easily by players twice his size and weight. At that level, you need to have

"It concerned an unfortunate training ground injury suffered by Marcus Stewart, who broke his cheekbone after a collision with Pablo. I remember it well. We were playing a five-a-side game and, in that kind of frenetic environment, it's all about sharp, quick reflexes."

more than skill and speed in your armoury – it's vital to be muscular, too.

For me, that signing was a misjudgement. Burley went for a player who just couldn't handle the physical side of the game. I was used to his training regime by now and, although his sessions were extremely hard, they benefited me for the rest of my career. He made me fitter and stronger than I'd ever been before. He knows how to improve players, which is exactly what he did with me, and his philosophy was that if you weren't fit enough for his training you clearly weren't good enough to play for Ipswich. I spoke about it earlier in the book and that's what nearly happened in my first pre-season at the club, when I underestimated the training routines. Each year he improved me and I truly want to thank him for that, although this particular campaign was a different experience for all of us because of our relegation.

While those signings were not exactly raging successes, Pablo Counago – who was to have two spells with the club and will be discussed later in the book – also joined in the summer of 2001. We became very good friends but there was one incident early in his first season which, perhaps above all others, highlighted our newfound fame as high-profile Premier League footballers. It concerned an unfortunate training ground injury suffered by Marcus Stewart, who broke his cheekbone after a collision with Pablo. I remember it well. We were playing a five-a-side game and, in that kind of frenetic environment, it's all about sharp, quick reflexes. Every player is desperate to win. The pair of them were on opposite sides and, during the match, a ball came in that Stewy tried to head. Pablo wanted to clear it, because he was defending. It was unclear whether Stewy's head was too low or Pablo's boot too high, but the upshot was that Pablo hit him full in the face.

There was nothing malicious in it and I can remember him apologising, but somehow it got in the press that they'd had a huge bust-up at the training ground. It was blown out of all proportion, just because the two of them were competing for the same position up front. Admittedly, they weren't the best of friends but in a squad of that size you can't expect everyone to get on famously. It's the same in any office or work environment. The pair of them were both competing and working hard in training but news of this incident seemed to spread throughout the nation and one of the rumours flying around (of which there were many) was that they were punching each other in the face. That wasn't the case at all. The irony was that while Stewy was starting every match with Pablo on the bench, it was Pablo who now had a chance while his rival was out injured.

> "After reading all those Wild West stories in the papers, it made me laugh how the press could make an elephant out of a fly (a Dutch saying, meaning to blow something out of proportion). I couldn't believe the fuss, because we were now high-profile Premier League footballers."

I know Pablo well, though. We're good mates and I can tell you he never intentionally wants to hurt someone. He is too good a player and professional to think like that. After reading all those Wild West stories in the papers, it made me laugh how the press could make an elephant out of a fly (a Dutch saying, meaning to blow something out of proportion). I couldn't believe the fuss but suppose it was a sign of the times, because we were now high-profile Premier League footballers. At that level, everything is world news and put under the microscope.

As for the season itself, I always think of it as one I'd rather forget – both on a personal note and for the club. I was barely involved in the first three or four games, which was so frustrating, especially as I'd done so much to get in shape. I tried to work as hard as possible in training, but for whatever reason I kept getting overlooked by the manager, who favoured Chris Makin (who had joined us late the previous season). Ironically, my first start came in our game up at Old Trafford in September and we were hammered 4-0. Then I was back on the bench and it felt like I was the scapegoat.

On the plus side, we were back in Europe and I was on the bench for our first game, at home to Torpedo Moscow. The second leg out in Russia provided me with some of my favourite memories of my time at Town. I'd never been to Moscow before

full english

but what an experience that was, visiting all the famous and historical places like the Red Square. It was freezing cold and I've got photos of myself and some of the other lads posing in traditional Russian hats (what the pictures don't show is that Richard Naylor – being a madman – was wearing shorts). Being able to explore such a big and exciting city was great, but in terms of the match itself I was to experience more frustration.

The day before the game we trained at the stadium and it was absolutely huge. It really felt we'd 'arrived' as we went through our paces, training for a big European night inside such a great arena. In reality, there was very little interest from the Russian fans – the crowd was only something like 10,000 in a 70,000 stadium (and a fair few of them were from Ipswich). We won 2-1, taking us through to the next round, but I was an unused substitute again and my sense of frustration and resentment was beginning to fester.

In the next round we played Swedish side Helsingborgs. The first game, at Portman Road, was a very lame, uneventful 0-0 draw. Then, in the return match, I experienced probably my lowest moment in an Ipswich shirt. In the build-up, Burley was struggling to decide whether to pick Makin or me. It was fairly obvious he was finding it hard to choose and, although he eventually plumped for me, I could sense he was less than convinced. Things just weren't right and, even after making his decision, he kept picking on me during the final training session. Basically, I couldn't do anything right and every time

I touched the ball I could hear him screaming at me from the sidelines. It just didn't add up. In my eyes, if you pick a player for your team it's best to support and encourage them, to give them confidence for the game. Burley went the other way. He chose me, then seemingly did everything possible to deflate me and try and make me feel inferior. I strongly got the feeling he regretted his decision.

Nevertheless, he kept me in the side and I felt I was doing alright during the game. Like most players, I'm my own worst critic and would hold my hands up if I was having a nightmare. On this occasion, though, I really thought I was doing OK. It was nothing spectacular from either the team or me but we were doing a decent job. Burley was on my back right from the start again, though. All I could hear was his voice, screaming every time I got near the ball.

> "At one point I snapped. We were losing 1-0 and I turned round and said angrily 'what do you want me to do?' As soon as the words left my mouth, I knew I'd done the wrong thing."

At one point I snapped. We were losing 1-0 and I turned round and said angrily 'what do you want me to do?' As soon as the words left my mouth, I knew I'd done the wrong thing. Within a few seconds, I looked back at the dugout and could see the fourth official getting the substitutes' board out. Then, when I checked again, the digit 'two' – my number – was emblazoned on the screen. And there were only 37 minutes on the clock. A sickening feeling of despair washed through me. Why me and why so soon before half-time? Why not make the change during the interval? To my mind, our situation had become personal and he was making a point. He'd embarrassed me (there

Above: Check out these hats - myself, Martijn Reuser, Richard Naylor and Jamie Clapham get in the spirit of things during our memorable trip to Moscow.

Left: Strained relations – George and myself exchanged words during our UEFA Cup match in Helsingborgs.

can't be many worse feelings as a player than being subbed before half-time) and not least because the game was being screened live on TV back in England. I couldn't believe what was happening and, feeling a mixture of bewilderment and rage, stormed past the dug out, down the tunnel and into the dressing room. Then I sat with my head in my hands, alone and contemplating the situation.

The game itself turned out to be a big success for the team. We won 3-1, and afterwards, there were quite a few fans staying in our hotel. Everyone gathered in the bar, preparing for a celebration, but I wasn't exactly in the party mood. Far from it. I was angry, upset and disillusioned and, after a drink or two, steeled myself to confront Burley. I politely asked him for a quiet word, then questioned why he'd decided to take me off so early. My words fell on deaf ears, though, because all I got in reply was 'we'll speak about it when we're back in England'.

There wasn't a lot I could say or do at that moment but I kept him to his word and, during our first training session back home, I levelled the same question at him again. Burley was furious. 'You weren't doing what I told you to do and I decide when I'm going to bring a player off' came the frosty response. I have to say the red mist descended and our conversation soon escalated into a full scale row. I had a real go back, complaining about

his criticism and lack of faith in me. He retaliated with the cutting line that I had been given a chance – but I'd 'blown it'. The whole thing got way out of hand. We were literally screaming at each other and all the other players, out on the training pitch, could see and hear everything. I stormed into the dressing room, knowing that my already strained relationship with the gaffer had plummeted to a new low. It was therefore no surprise that I wasn't even on the bench for our next game at Chelsea.

That was a horrible chapter of my Ipswich career. In fact, I shudder to think about it. The vast majority of my time at Ipswich was happy and positive – but that was a lonely and very bleak experience. I got a slight reprieve when I was back on the bench for our huge UEFA Cup tie at home to Inter Milan (although that was probably only because we were allowed to name seven subs), but overall I was very low. I was working hard and giving my all in training, but myself and the boss weren't speaking. We literally didn't say a word to each other for ages and the tension was unbearable. It would be the same in any job, if the boss and one of his employees weren't on speaking terms. I'd been such a key member of the team since joining and always felt an integral part of everything we achieved. Now I felt nothing more than an outcast. I was being frozen out and that was very hard to accept.

full english

Difficult times – even with players like Matt Holland **(above)** and Marcus Stewart, as he takes on Roy Keane **(below)**, plus new signings like Marcus Bent **(left)**, we ended the 2001-02 season being relegated from the Premier League.

Sometimes Burley would even drag me off during a training match and replace me at right-back. As you can imagine, that was awkward, even a little embarrassing at times (although, in fairness, I could see what a tremendous player he still was, solid as a defender and getting some great whip on his crosses into the box. He was incredibly fit and still in great shape).

I still got occasional chances, although they were few and far between. I remember being on the bench for a 0-0 draw with Middlesbrough, then getting a very rare start in a League Cup tie at Newcastle (Alan Shearer was unbelievable, scoring twice in a 4-1 victory). A young Darren Bent grabbed our consolation, underlining his vast potential, but for me it was another miserable night – and again it was all my fault, according to Burley. As with the Manchester United game, I felt like the scapegoat and my punishment was not even making the bench – even though seven subs were allowed again – for our historic return trip to Milan. Ten thousand ecstatic fans made the trip to the San Siro. They were singing and dancing throughout the entire match and for them it was a truly unforgettable experience. Christian Vieri absolutely murdered us with the three goals he scored that night. We never really stood a chance because after our win against them in the first leg, they really upped their game. I watched the match from the stands with the players' wives and felt helpless.

As the season progressed, my sense of isolation grew. I felt I wasn't needed and another huge kick in the teeth was heading my way when we travelled to Dagenham and Redbridge of all teams, for an FA Cup third-round tie in the January. On paper at least, this was a game I really fancied my chances in. We knew the manager was going to make wholesale changes, which he did, and I felt sure he'd give me a break. In many ways, it was now or never. If I didn't get a chance in a match like this then I couldn't see myself playing for the club again.

I travelled with the rest of the squad down to Victoria Road in a very positive mood – only to be hit with the bombshell that I wasn't even on the bench. To not make the team was one thing but to miss out on a substitute role was the final straw. Come on now! I was mortified. In my eyes, Burley had a golden opportunity to hand me the olive branch but instead showed once and for all that I wasn't part of his plans. It didn't seem to matter what I did. I was staying behind to do extra training, spending more time in the gym and trying as hard as I could to be as professional as possible in very difficult circumstances. However, nothing made the slightest difference.

I was so low and, once again, decided to have words. I braced myself for another confrontation in his office and told him that he might as well put me on the transfer list. His simple response was 'OK'. That said it all really and, as I trudged out, I was left with the overwhelming feeling that I'd never feature for Ipswich again. My time was up and I had to move on. I made it so easy for him. I probably should have asked to go on loan, to show him I'd fight to stay at this club by doing well elsewhere and to prove that I was still a good player he could depend on. However, I kind of put the word 'OK' in his mouth. The moment I made my request about the transfer list, I knew the answer straight away. Not a smart move Fab! I was on decent money at the time but, as far as I was concerned, it counted for nothing if I wasn't playing. I wanted to earn and justify my salary but if it meant taking a cut

to play for a different team then so be it. Nothing materialised in terms of a move but there was interest from several clubs, including Fulham and Manchester City.

In the meantime, it was hard to carry on as normal. I still had to travel with the team home and away, which meant training and preparing as if I was playing. I'd go through the usual routine, like being with the boys in the hotel and having a pre-match meal, only to have minimal involvement when kick-off rolled round. The fact the team were struggling rubbed salt into an already gaping wound. I could have accepted not being able to break into a winning, all-conquering side, but to hardly get a chance when things were going badly was doubly demoralising.

To be fair, I did make a handful of appearances after that meeting in the office but it was still a hard and pressured time, both for the team and me. By that stage, we were looking doomed for relegation and, all round, it was a turbulent year. The manager used me very sparingly and only when he really had to. Our finish to the season was abysmal and just one win in our last 13 games was well and truly relegation form, ending our brief but wonderful flirtation with the Premier League. To be honest, with a record like that, we didn't deserve to stay up but it was still hard to swallow, especially having enjoyed such unprecedented success the season before. One last strange twist of fate was that UEFA handed us a wildcard to play in the following season's UEFA Cup, due to our success in their Fair Play League. I think we were third overall, behind Manchester United and Arsenal, but could compete in Europe again because they'd already qualified for the Champions League. Talk about a bizarre end to the season.

full english

Sapped of confidence – my lack of opportunities in the team put me on a low ebb. Pictured here with Alan Lee.

For me, there were several reasons for our decline but one, as I touched on earlier, were the new faces. The whole feel of the club changed and the sense of banter and camaraderie evaporated. The season before we'd been a team on and off the pitch, not to mention the fact we were also very good friends. Now, we had players who, to be honest, were only playing for themselves – like Matteo and Finidi. It sounds harsh to say that and I liked them both as people, but they weren't good for the team. They certainly didn't make the side better or drive us forward. As was rumoured at the time, there was an issue in terms of what those guys were earning, too. There was a big gap between their salaries and those of the players that had got the club promoted in the first place. I believe they were on twice as much as some of the lads and that, understandably, caused much resentment. It would have been easier to accept if they'd come in and made a big difference, by contributing more to our team. That just wasn't the case, though, and the money issue caused bad feeling in the camp. Many a time in training arguments would erupt, tackles would fly in and sometimes even little fights would break out.

Suddenly, there was a host of different nationalities at the club and that led to a clash of cultures. The mix just didn't work and we had too many lads who wanted to be on their own, rather than bonding and gelling with their team-mates. That, undoubtedly, had a negative effect.

On the flip side to the signings, we lost arguably our best and most important player that summer in Richard Wright. He was such a huge influence and got us out of jail on so many occasions. The chance to join Arsenal was such a huge opportunity for him though, and while it left a void in our squad, no one could blame him for grabbing the chance to move to Highbury, especially if it was going to boost his chances with England. In addition to his crucial saves, we also really missed his sense of authority, organisation and communication with the back four. In many ways, we went from one extreme to the other because suddenly we had an Italian between the posts who hardly spoke any English.

Confidence – or rather a lack of it – was another factor. From my own point of view, I had a terrible season and never reached the heights and form of the previous year. Part of that, I'm sorry to say because he'd done brilliantly in his previous years as manager, was down to the gaffer. If you give a player confidence you'll get the best out of them. If you knock it out of them, as happened with me, then obviously they're going to struggle and feel low. In any line of work, it's hardly healthy when the boss and an employee aren't speaking. Before I'd always looked forward to training and never, ever thought of it as work. Now it was exactly that – something I had to do, get done and then get home again.

It was an incredibly hard time for so many reasons and we all went our separate ways that summer, licking our wounds from the ordeal of the campaign and hurt by relegation. From both a personal and team point of view, I found it impossible to be confident or upbeat and my worst fear was the prospect of more of the same during 2002-03. To my eternal gratitude, though, the exact opposite happened. From having one foot out the door, I was about to be given a whole new lease of life that resuscitated my ailing Ipswich career.

a change of boss

So many things were weighing me down and troubling me during the summer of 2002. I had a very young family – two little ones under the age of two – and we were spending a lot of time travelling back and forward to Holland. The children were obviously tiring (if immensely satisfying, as any dad will tell you), but the main thing getting me down was my insecurity at Ipswich. I honestly thought I was on my way out and that, as you can imagine, was extremely unsettling.

In that situation, you find yourself waiting for a phone call, knowing one conversation could mean you moving to a new club, new country or, in extreme cases, new continent. That, in turn, meant a new manager, new team-mates, new fans to win over – it was a huge concept to digest and so little wonder the prospect was never far from my mind. I reached a decision. I was heading into the last year of my contract and, as far as I was concerned, it was down to me once again to prove I was worthy of playing at this level. I was determined to win the manager over once and for all and was very focused on my mission to prove him wrong. I was hurting inside (perhaps I knew it was a losing battle) and my head was spinning in training, because that's when I was most fired up and thinking about what I wanted to achieve. Another player might have given up and demanded a move but I didn't want to feel pushed out. It was down to me to put things right.

Time for a change – chairman David Sheepshanks and the Town board decided to relieve George Burley of his duties in October 2002.

Despite my determination, I again started the season very much a fringe player. As before, that hurt because the team were struggling. Nevertheless, despite our problems, I never thought George Burley would lose his job. People have asked me whether I was hoping that would happen but I can honestly say it never entered my head. I thought he'd ride the storm and, given Ipswich's reputation for staying loyal to their managers (not to mention the fact he's a legend there from his playing days), I really didn't see it coming. Ipswich aren't known as a club that sack managers (although they've recently done just that by dismissing Jim Magilton). My view at the time was that they thrive on everything being settled and calm and always give their boss time to get things back on an even keel. Patience is key – except in this instance when it finally ran out.

full english

a change of boss

"It must have been an incredibly hard and upsetting time for Burley. His pride was severely dented and, despite the breakdown in my own relationship with him, I sympathised. After all, he was the manager who brought me to England in the first place, showed faith (in the beginning) and gave me a platform to go on and enjoy ten wonderful years at Ipswich."

Bad luck – despite the effort from all the players the results didn't go in Burley's favour.

Left: Under pressure – time was running out for Burley.

Left: Agony – Hermann's injury meant that this was his last game for Town against Stoke City, before his move to Charlton.

full english

New man in charge – Tony Mowbray took over as caretaker manager after Burley's departure.

Rare goal – Celebrating my goal against Rotherham in December.

It must have been an incredibly hard and upsetting time for Burley. His pride was severely dented and, despite the breakdown in my own relationship with him, I sympathised. After all, he was the manager who brought me to England in the first place, showed faith (in the beginning) and gave me a platform to go on and enjoy ten wonderful years at Ipswich. I'm sorry about the way things turned out but – and maybe he would even admit this now – it was probably the right decision for everyone.

My view is that he'd taken the team as far as he possibly could and it was time for him to do something different. He needed a fresh challenge and the fact that he's now in charge of the Scotland team shows his career has continued to go from strength to strength. Looking back, Burley would probably admit he made mistakes during his time at Ipswich (I'm sure the same applies to any manager). He undoubtedly signed players who didn't contribute enough to the team, as I've already discussed. The dressing room camaraderie and spirit dwindled and we became a weaker side, rather than building and becoming stronger.

Football can be a cruel game, though, and there's no mercy for either managers or players. In many ways it's a 'dog eat dog' situation and that's why, if I'm being brutally honest, I was relieved at the time of Burley's sacking. I know that sounds insensitive and, as I've said, as the years have slipped by, I've become more sympathetic and philosophical.

At the time, though, I was a very frustrated and disillusioned footballer – my career was ebbing away, I was on borrowed time at the club and I genuinely feared for my future. That's why a change of gaffer could only be a positive move for me – things could only get better. Towards the end of Burley's reign, I'd very much become a squad man who might get the occasional run-out if they were lucky but rarely trusted with a coveted spot in the starting line-up. That's why my ears and eyes pricked up when news broke of his departure.

The first inkling I got was when I received a text message from a friend, saying he'd heard a rumour on the grapevine. He suggested I would be really pleased (which, in truth, I was). Then

David Sheepshanks phoned everyone to confirm the news that Burley was going after a poor run of form and that Tony Mowbray would be taking charge in a caretaker role, starting with our next home game against Sheffield Wednesday. I'll be honest – for me personally, it was a great day. I saw it as a chance to forge a fresh start and all of the tension and animosity that had been brewing inside me suddenly lifted. I vowed to relax and start enjoying myself again.

Mogga took charge of the team for four games and did a reasonable job (one win and two draws), but it soon became obvious the board were looking for a more experienced man to steer the club forward. Mogga, for all his vast experience and success as an inspirational player, was only just cutting his teeth in terms of coaching and, on this occasion, the job came too soon. There were so many applications for the post and understandably so. After all, this was a team that had only just suffered relegation from the Premier League. The ground, training facilities and fan-base were top-class and, perhaps crucially, we were still receiving parachute payments after dropping out of the top flight. In other words, we were still a very attractive proposition and any out of work manager, I'm sure, would have jumped at the chance to take over.

> "I'll be honest – for me personally, it was a great day. I saw it as a chance to forge a fresh start and all of the tension and animosity that had been brewing inside me suddenly lifted. "

From a players' perspective, everyone was right behind Mogga. I knew him well, obviously, as a friend and team-mate, and knew he had all the required attributes to be a top manager. Certain players are always destined to go down that route. They're calm, intelligent and real thinkers when it comes to football. Mogga definitely fitted that bill and so did the likes of Veno and Jim. Of the current crop of Town players, David Wright stands out as a manager for the future. He's sensible and articulate and you know he has a huge understanding of the game. On this occasion, it wasn't to be for Mogga. The board decided he wasn't experienced enough and, although he was bitterly disappointed to be overlooked, maybe it was a blessing in disguise.

From a caretaker manager with very little experience, Town really went for someone from the opposite end of the spectrum when they appointed Joe Royle. What a great and very astute decision that turned out to be. From a team point of view, he was just the man to come in, steady the ship and point us back in the right direction. And from my own perspective, it was a dream scenario – my career was finally back on track. It's easy to say now, because of the way our relationship panned out, but I can honestly say I liked and warmed to Joe the first time I met him. He was a gentleman and a football legend with a warmth, charm and sense of humour that made him hugely endearing.

To the players, he soon became like a father figure and even those who weren't getting into his team still liked him a lot. He addressed all of us fairly and politely (although he paid particular

full english

Right: Getting shirty - Joe Royle poses for the customary shots after being confirmed as the next Ipswich boss.

Centre: Keeping fit – Juliette shows me how it's done during one of her Pilates sessions.

attention to the strikers, given that he used to be one. In the nicest and most professional way, he was always on at the likes of Darren Bent and Shefki Kuqi, because he knew he could help and develop them. He always thought they could do better). His man-management skills were second to none and so many people could watch and learn from the way he conducted himself around his players. I'll never forget his first team meeting. It was inspirational and really got us believing again, because he was convinced there was enough time left to revive our season.

My first one-on-one meeting was equally uplifting because he told me that, as far as he was concerned, I was starting from scratch. "What's happened has happened – it's in the past now," he said and I remember being really surprised and impressed by how much he knew about me already. He said I'd always played well against his Manchester City sides and then threw down the gauntlet, telling me he was giving me a fresh chance – now it was down to me to take it. It's amazing how quickly things can change and I'm a strong believer in fate. One decision – the hiring or firing of a manager – can make or break a player's career. I was still the same footballer that I'd always been but now, at long last, I had a fresh chance and that was a huge source of motivation. The opportunity to rebuild my career was a real spur and, mentally, I felt as positive and buoyant as I had for ages. To tell the truth, I was buzzing again and what a wonderful feeling that was, after all the doom and gloom.

Willie Donachie's arrival as Joe's assistant was another huge milestone, both for the team and me. The pair of them reignited my career overnight. They were very different men – which is probably why they worked so well in tandem – but both were very calm and methodical. Willie was a class act and very much in tune with my philosophies about fitness, diet and so on. He introduced me to yoga, which I've done ever since and is something I attribute towards the longevity of my career. For that, I'm really thankful to Willie. I've always been open-minded about things like that and think that if anything

Bent double – the two Bents, Darren and Marcus.

can improve your game by even half a percent then it's worth doing. People like Tommy Miller, Richard Naylor and the goalkeepers (particularly useful to them) were also very enthusiastic. Others, like Jim, were far from convinced and that's fair enough, too. These things aren't for everyone. It's very much a personal decision but, if ever I move into management, it's certainly an option I'd give my players.

During Joe and Willie's time, it was normal practice to have hour-long yoga sessions, usually before training on a Monday. Personally, I found it great and am a firm believer that, as a modern day footballer, it's vital to be flexible and supple. Old-fashioned stretching exercises are still useful but not enough and I think part of the reason I've had a relatively injury-free career (certainly in terms of long-term problems) was down to things like that. Like any sportsman, I had niggles from time to time but nothing major – I've always been aware and open-minded about the best ways to look after and maintain my body. People see us out on the pitch but possibly don't understand the various things we have to do to ensure our fitness is as high as possible. Training is obviously the main thing but all these other bits and pieces help.

The very first yoga session – which was totally optional – did, admittedly, feel a little strange. It was hard not to feel just a little self-conscious but I soon got into it and started feeling the benefits straight away. I knew it was paying off and that's why I was so determined to continue with it. Juliette teaches Pilates and that's another thing I've always enjoyed and benefited from (although I'm sure she'd say I'm her nightmare pupil. I always make comments and ask lots of questions and sometimes, with a smile on her face, she turns on me and says 'just

get on with it!'). I'm also a big believer in massages – it's something I've always had during my time in England. They usually last for about an hour and a half and, at the time, can be extremely painful, but the feeling afterwards is great and makes you feel so much better.

We eventually finished seventh in the table which, although disappointing in terms of the play-offs, was a fair achievement, given our dreadful start. There were lots of highlights along the way, too, and for me the big one was scoring at Carrow Road. As everyone knows, I didn't net too many times during my Town career but how fortunate to be able to say I scored goals against Manchester United and Norwich.

The derby game really sticks out in my mind and not just because of the goal. It was such a tense affair because aside from the obvious rivalry, we were up there pushing for promotion. We desperately needed the points to stay in touch and because there was so much at stake you could really feel the edge and emotion. Both sides had chances so it was such an amazing feeling to put us in front. Dean Bowditch had just stepped off the bench and I remember he started the move down the left. One of our defenders – I can't remember who – broke forward and got a cross in, which was headed away by a Norwich player. There I was in a perfect position to have a crack at goal. I controlled it first, then managed to send my volley exactly where I wanted to – into the corner of the goal. What a feeling. If I say so myself, it was a brilliant finish which I'll always be proud of and the sense of elation was overwhelming, especially as I was in front of our fans.

It was a very special moment and lots of people have asked me how the feeling compared

full english

to scoring against United. The honest answer is that I couldn't pick a favourite. Both are firmly up there as career highlights and both were fantastic moments during huge occasions. One difference between the two is how I felt during the remainder of the respective matches. After my wild celebrations against United, I found it easy to put the goal to the back of my mind and stay focused on my main job for the evening – defending against a rampant and imposing United side. Against Norwich, on the other hand, I must admit I kept replaying the goal over and over in my mind. I probably still had a smile on my face and found it difficult to concentrate on anything else for the remaining 18 minutes. I'll certainly never forget them both and the important thing, in terms of the Norwich strike, was that it paved the way to a crucial victory. I had a strong feeling that whoever scored first would go on to win the game and so, after scoring our first goal, you could say I was the unlikely hero. Darren Bent added a second and then it really was party time. I'd played my part in a famous victory and no one can ever take that special feeling away from me.

The home game against Sheffield United is another one firmly embedded in my mind. Joe has referred to it since as his favourite match as Ipswich manager and I agree that it was an unbelievable afternoon – partly because of the drama within the game and partly because of the deafening atmosphere inside Portman Road. The crowd were so behind us and the noise and support they generated was a major factor in the final result. Things didn't start well when Pablo Counago was sent off after just 20 minutes. Down to ten men that early in the game, we had to work hard to retain our shape and keep going but, when we went two-down, I think everyone thought it wasn't going to be our day.

The face says it all - Tommy Miller and myself wildly celebrate my famous goal at Carrow Road.

full english

Catch me if you can – the likes of Darren Bent and Tommy give chase as I speed towards the jubilant Town fans.

However, we somehow summoned the strength and energy to get back and two goals from Benty and one from Darren Ambrose capped an amazing comeback and a fitting result, given that an air of sadness had overshadowed our pre-match build-up following the sad death of Dale Roberts.

Dale had been battling Non-Hodgkins Lymphoma but lost his courageous and dignified fight in the days leading up to the Blades game. When he passed away, it was a sad moment in the history of Ipswich Town. His funeral, which the whole squad attended, was very emotional and there were also lots of old Town players there who played under Dale. We also played a testimonial match against Newcastle United and all the proceeds went to his family. I was particularly upset by his death, having played so regularly in his reserve side the season before. We'd won the league title that year and, I can safely say, the boys did it for Dale (the

Party time - myself, Tommy and Benty let our hair down at Carrow Road.

I'm in there somewhere! - I can hardly breathe as the boys pile on top of me in front of our fans at Norwich.

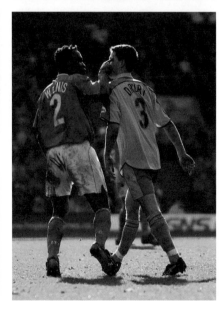

full english

Gone but never forgotten – Dale Roberts' death was particularly hard for his very good friend and former team-mate George Burley. Myself, Martijn Reuser, skipper Matt Holland and Andy Marshall arrive for his funeral.

same applied for the Sheffield United result). It was impossible not to be impressed by him. In those final weeks he was getting more ill and weak by the day. Everyone knew the inevitable was not far away but you'd never have guessed from his mood. To his very great credit, he tried as hard as humanly possible to retain his bubbly, upbeat and outgoing personality. He must have felt so dreadful and frightened inside but, in terms of his public front, couldn't have been more brave or inspiring.

The vast majority of people would, understandably, be very down and scared if they were diagnosed with cancer. Dale was the opposite and, in many ways, I think football and coaching was a welcome distraction from the turmoil going on in his private life. He took the attitude that there was no point sitting at home moping and it was certainly good to see him at training and games. It made us even more determined to get a positive result and it was something we talked about in the dressing room. The lads were united in their respect for him and there was very much an attitude of 'let's do it for Dale'.

Despite those victories and a real revival under Joe, we just missed out on the play-offs

and, as people will remember, the latter part of the season was also an awkward time because the club had a spell in administration. After the big signings the previous year, followed by relegation, it was in serious trouble. At the time, when we were in the Premier League, I don't think anyone could foresee what would happen the following year. The club had invested heavily on new players and, in recent years, had also revamped two of their stands - the South Stand, better known as the Greene King Stand, and the North Stand. Extra capacity and modernisation were the reasons behind the rebuilds but the work came at a heavy price.

The club were hoping to establish and maintain a Premier League team so they would benefit from the vast riches of top-flight football and not least the mega-millions being pumped in by Sky TV. However, after our brilliant first year followed by the disaster of relegation, the club faced an uphill struggle to pay the players' wages and, of course, the repayments for the stands. The only thing they could do was offload the highest earners and/or sell their most prized assets (I should add that despite those financial issues, in all my years playing for the club they were never late paying my wages).

Paying our respects - the players hang their heads and remember a truly great man during the minute's silence for Dale.

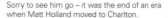

Sorry to see him go – it was the end of an era when Matt Holland moved to Charlton.

The climax to the season signalled the end of another era because we said goodbye to Matty Holland (who moved on to Charlton). As I said earlier, he was a truly great player, captain and servant to Ipswich and his appearance record – hardly ever missing a game through injury – was extraordinary. Matt was a great guy and I was sorry to see him go but, despite him leaving and missing out on the play-offs, I still felt positive. My own career had obviously been revitalised and, once again, I felt great about my team-mates. The spirit and camaraderie had returned, thanks to Joe, and a real friendship and bond had developed between myself and the other foreigners – Martijn, Hermann Hreidarsson and Thomas Gaardsoe (who'd arrived the previous year but had only been a bit-part player under Burley). As pals and team-mates, we really clicked and, with our respective wives and girlfriends, spent an awful lot of time together, especially on Sundays.

Hermann and Ragna lived in the same road as us and had a Jacuzzi in their back garden, which was great on a cold day. We all used to sit and chat in it for ages. Thomas (a real dreamer but a lovely lad) and his girlfriend, Anne, lived in the house backing on to ours and he often joked about putting a gate

in the fence, so he could come round whenever he liked (I was quick to dismiss that idea – much as I liked him I wanted to retain some privacy). The eight of us went out a lot, had nice meals together and became very close. In fact, I'd say that in terms of feeling happy and settled, that was my favourite year at Ipswich.

As the older statesman, I was the one who always had to be sensible and responsible but was always creased up with laughter when Thomas and Hermann – two big kids – used to have their legendary play-fights. They were both such well-built, muscular lads and it was always a running joke as to which of them was the strongest – much of our time together invariably descended into a big play-fight where they'd be wrestling around one of our lounges, trying to grapple the other one to the floor.

All in all, it was a wonderful year. We had a top manager and a very likeable, determined bunch of players. My mood that summer, compared to the previous one, had changed completely and it was impossible not to feel buoyant about the future – a future that, at one time, I never thought I'd experience as an Ipswich player.

full english

so near and yet so far

With my mood so upbeat, I had a great summer and was safe in the knowledge that I had at least one more year at the club, having signed a new contract in April. Of course, it would have been nice to have the security of a longer deal but at least this way I knew I had to perform and be on top of my game, determined to win another contract towards the end of the following season. It was definitely a source of motivation, although I'd be lying if I said it played on my mind that much. As far as I was concerned, my professionalism meant I always wanted to play to the top of my capability and if I did that then I was fairly sure a new deal would take care of itself. As for the one I'd just signed, I was as confident as I could be that the club would offer me something new. Despite the uncertainty of my career a few months previously, I'd become an established member of the squad and had a fantastic relationship with the manager – penning a new deal was my reward.

While I was most definitely staying, it was time for others to bid farewell. I saw so many players come and go during my time at the club and while some liked to arrange dos to properly say their goodbyes, others preferred to slip away quietly – effectively through the back door. Matteo and Finidi fell into the latter category and, to be fair, it's easy to see why. Neither of them had much success with the club. I doubt either of them really enjoyed their time with us and neither ever gelled with the other lads. Their exits were both bound to be low profile.

On the flip side, we welcomed some fresh faces, including new goalkeeper Kelvin Davis, who joined from Wimbledon. Kelvin arrived just before the season began and, from day one in training, I knew we were on to a winner. He had such a brilliant kick and I've never seen a keeper capable of kicking a ball so sweetly or precisely. He was a top man to have between the posts – imposing, communicative and a very safe pair of hands (even if he was the most dreadful outfield player when we messed around in training). Kelvin was also a really nice and friendly guy – albeit a complete nutter. I'd say he and Kevin Horlock, who I'll talk about later, were my funniest, most outrageous team-mates at Ipswich. Kelvin was an absolute scream, so witty and sarcastic and constantly winding people up and taking the mickey. I thought he was great and a brilliant personality and character to bring into the squad, filling the dressing room with a very positive and happy atmosphere. I must share one little Kelvin story, which, to this day, still makes me laugh. The boys had just made their way out on to the training pitch when we heard a noise from behind us. We looked round and there he was wearing nothing but his socks, boots, pants and gloves – jogging out and ready to start training. We were in stitches and the mental image still makes me chuckle. It was typical Kelvin.

Soon to be team-mates - Pablo Counago celebrates scoring at Turf Moor, much to the disgust of future team-mate Drissa Diallo.

Georges Santos was another new arrival and he joined us while we were away on tour that summer. Again, my first impression was very positive. In fact, I thought he was brilliant – ridiculously strong and good in the air. I'm not really sure why things never worked out for him. It was strange because he came with a hard-man image (his disciplinary record was appalling) but his personality was the exact opposite. On the pitch, he was a big, snarling and uncompromising warrior. Off it, he wore glasses and was almost unrecognisable – quiet, softly spoken and deeply intelligent.

Joe clearly felt our defence needed bolstering because he also snapped up Drissa Diallo, from Burnley. It was quite funny because the season before Pablo had had a bust up with him, during our match at Turf Moor. The pair of them had clashed and I think Pablo still has the scar on his head to prove it. I'm sure it was entirely accidental but I remember Pablo bled very heavily at the time. In a fit of rage, he'd flown back at Drissa and now, six months later, they were about to become team-mates. I'm not sure how he felt when he first found out but I know he soon reached the conclusion it was better to have Drissa in his team than be against him, such was his physical and no-nonsense approach.

In terms of his football, Drissa was certainly wild. He wasn't the most skilful or graceful of players but compensated for it by way of endeavour and work-rate. Even in training, his competitiveness and will to win shone through, to the point that he flew in with meaty tackles – challenges the rest of us probably wouldn't make outside of a match situation. To Drissa, though, any match – from a Champions League final to a kick-about in training – simply had to be won and, while commendable, his sometimes over the top attitude wound up some of our strikers. On lots of occasions, one of his clattering challenges would be followed by a sharp exchange of words with the likes of Pablo, Alun Armstrong or Darren Bent. There were arguments and confrontations but Joe didn't mind. In fact, I think he liked it. He'd been a strong, physical striker during his playing days and he thought having a hard-man defender out on the training pitch would help toughen up his front men.

With our new signings settled and in place, everything looked so rosy as we kicked off for another season – confident and happy as a squad and oozing potential. Needless to say, hopes for promotion were once again sky high and there was a genuine feeling throughout the club that this

full english

would be our year. Sadly, our form for the first few games didn't exactly match those lofty expectations. In fact, our results in the first six games – four defeats and two draws - were more relegation form. The last game in that opening sequence was a 4-1 defeat at West Brom and Thomas Gaardsoe, having moved to The Hawthorns during the summer, scored one of their goals. What an utterly depressing day that was. I'd had my lows before but, from a team perspective, that run of results left me feeling as flat as I ever felt during my entire ten years at Portman Road.

I sensed a serious problem and started to doubt some of my team-mates. I remember being interviewed by one of the local journalists outside the ground and venting my frustrations about how the players needed to question themselves and take a long, hard look in the mirror. They were strong words but I meant every one of them and was just being honest, something I always tried to do when dealing with the Press. Questions kept rolling over in my mind as we started our drive home from the Midlands. As a team, were we working hard enough? Were the players hungry enough? And was the passion and desire there to get the club promoted?

It was horrible to be thinking that way, given the great expectations sweeping through the club just a few weeks previously, but I obviously wasn't alone in having those thoughts because on the Monday we assembled for a team meeting, led by Joe. As I said earlier, his man-management skills were second to none and as soon as he started talking he got the right response. Most of the time, Burley seemed to focus on his favoured players, his starting XI, but Joe had time for the whole squad. He encouraged and inspired those in his team, but also put a metaphorical arm round those who were knocking on the door.

The overwhelming message was that we were all in it together and it was down to all of us to put things right. No one had cause to feel isolated or excluded. It was just what the doctor ordered and provided a perfect platform to put our cards on the table, speak openly and honestly and iron out whatever problems had led to our dismal form. I certainly had my say and, overall, it was a very productive session. We debated what had gone wrong and how we could put things right and we all agreed we could work harder. We needed to sort out all the little extras, like tracking back and doing the ugly things, and if we could do that I felt confident our fortunes would change. I certainly retained my belief in the manager and players – it was just a question of taking this newfound inspiration into matches.

On a personal note, I'd certainly had a reality check. I could see what had been going wrong and was absolutely determined to put things right – for my own pride and that of my team-mates, but also out of a sense of duty for the manager. Joe had put such faith in me. He believed in me and had breathed fresh life into my career, so the very least I could do was repay him. After the debacle at The Hawthorns, it was great that we had another game so soon with Walsall due at Portman Road on the Tuesday. Thankfully, at long last, we managed our first win, although I remember that being a rather tense affair (a penalty from Alun and a second by Darren Bent helped us register our first three points). Nevertheless, we'd won the game and that, in the climate, was the main thing. Mentally, we were able to tick off the fact we'd won a match and it gave us a spur to finally get our season up and running.

To that end, we were soon helped by the fact three new faces arrived in quick succession – Shefki

Soaring through the air - Shefki Kuqi performs his legendary 'belly flop' goal celebration. If I attempted that I think I'd break every bone in my body!

Such a good feeling – myself and the boys celebrate another goal.

Kuqi, Alan Mahon and Chris Bart-Williams. All three arrived on loan and had a very positive impact, both on the pitch and off it. Chris was a curious individual, very likeable but also quite eccentric. He was heavily into his fashion and clothes, which I admired, but he did some funny things. One example that springs to mind is during a match, either his debut or second game, when Jim (then the captain) had to go off. Jim chucked the armband to Chris, who was then supposed to pass it to me. It was fairly obvious what he was supposed to do but, for whatever reason, he refused to hand it over – and instead put it on his arm. So we finished the game with a loanee – having only been at the club a matter of days – as our self-appointed skipper.

Alan was a top man and, I have to admit, I've always had a soft spot for Irish people. As well as my team-mates (Alan Lee, Owen Garvan and Shane Supple, to name but three), I've been to Dublin a few times and I always find the locals full of charm. They're very friendly, open and generous and Alan was no different.

Shefki was another hugely likeable person and soon became great pals with his room-mate,

Tommy Miller. Shefki was a fairly quiet man but very good in the group. He wasn't a big joker like some of the others but one thing he did do which was both mad and outrageous was his incredible belly-flop goal celebration. I'll never forget the first time I saw him do it, on his debut at Watford. His leap was astonishing and he executed the whole thing so gracefully, telling me afterwards that he didn't feel a thing when he came down to land. If I tried doing it I'd probably break every bone in my body and be out for about three seasons.

Shefki rapidly became a fans' favourite and it's easy to see why, because of his all-action, bustling style but also because of his work-rate and commitment. He was a very fit man – him and Matt Richards always came out on top when we did the bleep tests in training – and I loved the way he huffed and puffed and gave everything for 90 minutes. Whatever the situation in the game, whether we were winning, drawing or losing, he'd run around like a headless chicken, tracking back and often chasing lost causes. It was a great quality to have and little wonder the supporters appreciated his efforts so much.

full english

The tone of our dressing-room meeting, allied with the new loan arrivals, certainly had a profound effect because our fortunes improved dramatically. After West Brom, we won eight games out of nine, with the only defeat being a 3-2 reverse at Sunderland (where we never seemed to get anything). A winning mentality had replaced the losing habit and, slowly but surely, we started climbing our way up the table. Our pre-season aims had been realistic but it was only now, well into the campaign, that we were starting to match them.

One match that sticks in my mind was our FA Cup tie with Derby County, then managed by George Burley. The result was very pleasing as we won 3-0. However, what made it memorable for me was the fact I captained the side. I felt so proud because not only had I worked my way back to being a regular in the team but now here I was wearing the skipper's armband. It felt so special. I had a nice chat with Burley in the hallway before going into the referee's room an hour before kick-off. The four match officials, myself, Joe, Burley and Ian Taylor, the Derby captain, went through the team sheets.

When Burley was at Ipswich, I wasn't a regular and often found myself on the bench or in the stands during his final year in charge. Look at me now - just a year and a half later I was captain of the very same club with a new boss who had shown every faith in me. It just goes to show how much influence a manager can have on your career. I don't feel any anger towards Burley, though. I haven't got an axe to grind and we actually got on really well in the following years. It was just that he preferred others ahead of me which, at the time, was very hard to swallow. Of course, these things happen in football, though, and I'll always be very grateful that he gave me the change to play in England. It's something I'll never forget.

There were decent wins in that little sequence, culminating in a thrilling 4-3 victory at Crystal Palace. My memories of the match itself are a little vague but I remember we conceded a late equaliser – then promptly went straight up the other end and grabbed a last-gasp winner through

Shefki. The celebrations afterwards were wonderful but, sadly, the momentum didn't last. Our form became a little more patchy and inconsistent after that and among our worst results was a 3-1 defeat against Norwich.

For the worst reasons, that game will always stick in my mind. The result was depressing enough but I also learnt a very valuable lesson in terms of giving interviews so soon after a game, when my emotions were still so raw. I was upset because we'd had most of the play and felt in control of the game. However, Norwich, at that time, had a knack of grinding out results when they weren't playing well. In my opinion, they were hardly spectacular. Fair play to them, that's what successful sides do and they were top of the league, which was a great achievement. I can see that now but, at the time, numb and smarting from our defeat, I said too much to a journalist.

I had just emerged from a very angry and disappointed dressing room, flooded with disbelief that we'd lost the game to our main rivals in such circumstances. To cap a miserable day for me personally, I'd also been booked and substituted after 72 minutes. It's fair to say I wasn't in a very good mood when I bumped into the reporter. I agreed to do an interview and, during the course of it, quite fairly, I was asked what I thought of Norwich. It was like a red rag to a bull. Being brutally honest, I said they were nothing special and that they'd been fortunate. I said I couldn't understand how we'd lost and then, pouring petrol on the fire, added that if they went up they'd have to buy a whole new team – or else they'd come straight back down. I'd normally think more carefully before saying something so provocative but, at that time, pure, raw emotion got the better of me.

As well as appearing in our local paper, my comments were also picked up by The Sun. As I held them both in front of me and relived the interview, I immediately regretted my comments. I'd made life very awkward and difficult for myself and, as my quotes filtered out into the public domain, I was soon to get a very frosty response from the Norwich fans. All the players have their own pigeonholes at the ground and I suddenly started getting lots of extra post. To start with I thought I must be really popular all of a sudden – but was in for a nasty surprise. Much of it was acceptable and understandable. The majority was just people getting defensive and sticking up for their team. People said it was just sour grapes and called me a crybaby. One person even cut out a picture of my head and stuck it on an image of a baby, with tears drawn streaming down my cheeks.

That was all quite odd and nothing I couldn't handle, but some of it was quite over the top. I got

> "However, Norwich, at that time, had a knack of grinding out results when they weren't playing well. In my opinion, they were hardly spectacular. Fair play to them. I can see that now but, at the time, numb and smarting from our defeat, I said too much to a journalist."

letters saying I was a dead man and threatening to break my arms and legs if I ever set foot in Norwich. At the time, it was really frightening. I didn't tell anyone about it, even Juliette. She knew my comments hadn't exactly been well received but the last thing I wanted was to frighten her by telling her I'd received death threats. I didn't report it to anyone at the club, either, or my room-mate and great friend, Martijn Reuser. I just wanted the whole thing to blow over as quickly as possible.

The honest truth is that I didn't understand the consequences of my actions. I was speaking openly and saying what I really felt, but sometimes perhaps honesty isn't the best policy – especially in the context of a football rivalry, where emotions run so high. It can backfire and come back to haunt you, as was the case with me. Overwhelmed by emotion, I was only saying what so many other people were probably thinking but, even so, it wasn't very clever and I learnt a valuable lesson, to be more cautious in future interviews. It's one thing to talk about your own team but quite another to start criticising others, especially your main rivals.

"It was like a red rag to a bull. Being brutally honest, I said they were nothing special and that they'd been fortunate. I said I couldn't understand how we'd lost and then, pouring petrol on the fire, added that if they went up they'd have to buy a whole new team – or else they'd come straight back down."

The great irony is that, to some extent, I was proved right because Norwich did come straight back down the following season, after just one year in the Premier League. Not that that gives me any satisfaction. I upset and offended some of their fans and for that I really am sorry. I think the dust has settled now, though. I've only been back there for football (before it was somewhere we'd been to visit, to do a bit of shopping) and won't risk doing anything else, especially if I'm with my family.

I was quite relieved we didn't have to play Norwich the following year, because they were in the Premier League. It was bad enough the season after, when they were back down, and the stick I got was unbelievable. Even before and after the game, driving to and from the ground, you could see the anger and venom in some fans' faces. They were baying for me but I just kept my headphones on and tried as hard as possible to ignore it. Then throughout the whole game it was Wilnis this and Wilnis that. They were taking the mickey out of my hair (which was braided at the time) and some people even spat at me. There was a temptation to react, but I didn't and I'm so glad I kept my cool. The one thing those fans wanted was for me to shout, spit or even fight back, but that would have led to horrendous problems which would have had very serious repercussions.

The only positive to come from the whole fiasco was that my popularity among Ipswich fans soared! They loved the fact one of their own was criticising the enemy and it made me a bit of a hero. The supporters even came up with a song, which became the theme tune for the rest of my time with the club. Even now, some people still sing 'Fabian Wilnis is a blue, is a blue, is a blue – he hates Norwich'. They chanted it at every opportunity and never more so than in that return match at Carrow Road. Whenever the Norwich fans taunted me, I could hear ours backing me up by roaring the anthem. Some of them even produced a banner – a great big white sheet with the words daubed in blue. After the game, when we were warming down, they asked me if I wanted to keep it but I politely declined. I thought the sight of me leaving with a banner over my shoulder would pour petrol on an already raging fire. It was quite sweet because around that time, Yasmin came up to me and said 'daddy, do you really hate Norwich?' Even Jada and Kaylee (then only five and six years old), having heard their classmates signing it at school, starting chanting it. I told them I didn't hate anyone and discouraged them from using such a strong word, especially as they were still so young and didn't really understand. I explained how much the derby match means to the fans and how important that sense of rivalry is to some of them.

"The only positive to come from the whole fiasco was that my popularity among Ipswich fans soared! They loved the fact one of their own was criticising the enemy and it made me a bit of a hero. The supporters even came up with a song, which became the theme tune for the rest of my time with the club."

After a season of success – both for the team and me personally – we eventually finished fifth and faced the lottery of the play-offs. Norwich and West Brom were the top two by far and deservedly booked their places in the top flight. For us, it was a two-legged affair against West Ham. I was proud of the season we'd had. My yoga and Pilates had done their job – keeping me flexible and supple and allowing me to play in the vast majority of games. I didn't have any injury worries of note and it was only a couple of suspensions that kept me on the sidelines. As for the team, things would have been so different had we started the season better. However, dropping so many points early on came back to haunt us and, rather than being up there in the top two, we had to prepare and keep going for those games against the Hammers.

The first leg was at a very noisy and pumped up Portman Road and, although we won 1-0, I remember being disappointed with the score. We'd been so on top and should have scored more than the one goal netted by Darren Bent. Benty himself had had a few chances but unfortunately couldn't take them and it meant we went to Upton Park protecting a very tricky 1-0 lead. Nevertheless, at least we'd won the game. It could have been a lot worse and we still felt confident heading into the second leg three days later. Unfortunately, though, things didn't go to plan. Alan Pardew, the West Ham manager, had wound our players up by saying we were in for a shock at Upton Park and that we wouldn't know what had hit us. Sadly, he did a great job and was probably right because I have to admit a lot of our players were intimidated by the crowd and noise.

full english

I've thought about it a lot since and, with hindsight, maybe there was something different in terms of atmosphere within the squad. I'd noticed something was amiss the night before the game, in our hotel, and there was an unmistakable air of tension.

As for the game, we never got going, failed to create any clear cut chances and lost 2-0. What disappointed me most, though, was the fact we allowed ourselves to be bullied. Too many players froze and were over-awed by the occasion and the hostile atmosphere, which meant we didn't do ourselves justice. West Ham fans can be a hard, intimidating bunch (I became even more aware of that during my year at Grays, in Hammers heartland) and, to be fair, the noise they generated that night was incredible. I remember before the game when they sang the famous 'Bubbles' song – it made the hairs on the back of my neck stand on end.

For me personally, I found it uplifting and was determined to silence them, but for others – especially the younger lads - it knocked them off their stride and affected their game. Even on the way to the match, the West Ham fans had done their job by successfully getting under the skin of our boys. As we looked out through the coach windows, the supporters were chanting at us and their snarling faces were a vision of hatred. They were screaming abuse at us. I tried to stay focused; to concentrate on the job in hand and play things over and over in my mind but it's definitely fair to say others were affected.

Looking back, the writing was probably on the wall after the first leg, even though we won. We hadn't been in great form and we lacked momentum. West Ham, in contrast, had enjoyed a storming end to the season and their form helped them nick one of the last play-off spots. They were buoyed and oozing confidence, whereas we were still licking our wounds at missing out on automatic promotion. To then lose in the play-offs was a hammer-blow (pardon the pun) and also a huge anti-climax. The coach journey home was excruciating – hardly anyone said anything and, as we snaked away from the ground, all we could see were home supporters jumping around, chanting and jeering at us. It was a sickening feeling because we knew we'd let ourselves down.

When we finally arrived back at Portman Road, everyone said their goodbyes, hopped in their cars and headed off to enjoy their respective summer breaks. That was that. Had things been different, we might have been planning and preparing for a trip to the Millennium Stadium. Instead, our season had been unceremoniously ended and there was nothing left to say or do. We just had to go our separate ways, flush the whole experience out of our systems and try and learn from our mistakes.

Getting over the defeat was easier said than done, though. Personally, I found it very hard and spent the first few weeks of my break repeatedly asking myself 'what if'. What if we'd started the season better? What if we'd taken our chances in the first leg at Portman Road? I suddenly had so much time to dwell and reflect and, much as I tried to move on, it wasn't easy because I was hurting. I certainly didn't want to watch the play-off final on TV. I couldn't care less who went up. The only thing that concerned me was the fact we weren't in Cardiff. And the only positive to come from that gut-wrenching feeling was a determination to do better the following season.

déjà vu

Although the following season was to end with a sickening feeling of deja vu, I've got happy memories of the summer of 2004. The agony of our play-off defeat a few weeks previously obviously rankled but, in time, the pain dwindled and we came round to a positive way of thinking. The flames of hunger and determination started to burn again and a few new faces in the dressing room only served to heighten those hopes and expectations.

New strike-force - after the transfer of so many proven players, Joe Royle tried to solve the problem by signing Nicky Forster and Sam Parkin

One of them was our new skipper, a natural leader and a brilliant defender in Jason De Vos, who for me was very much in the same mould as Tony Mowbray. We clicked straight away and I loved his intelligent, reasoned way of looking at things. He was so bright and well spoken and fitted in immediately, playing a huge part in our strong and convincing start to the season. With him on board, we were flying right from day one. Much of our success was down to our settled, well-balanced and resolute side and we were near the top of the league by Christmas.

Another of the other summer arrivals, who also made a very positive impact, ranks as another of my funniest and most entertaining team-mates – the joker that is Kevin Horlock. It's hard to emphasise just how amusing he was, other than to say that there were times when his gags and comments had the rest of us crying with laughter. He was a great one for practical jokes, too, and took great delight in doing daft things. On one occasion, after he'd left training for the day, a few of us were in the changing rooms when we noticed someone had been tampering with our socks. Danny Haynes was the first to notice – one sock was normal and the other had been cut, so his toes poked straight

out the end. Lewis Price and Shane Supple went to put theirs on and had the same problem and we all knew without hesitation who was responsible - Kev. We were all phoning and texting him but no one was upset. It probably sounds silly but little things like that always gave us a laugh and that's why dressing rooms are all the better for people like him.

Consistency was the key to our success in the first half of the season. We were flying and regularly picking up points, although only a few games really stand out in my mind. One was our 5-1 thumping of Sheffield United in early November and another was the 2-1 victory against fellow promotion-chasers Wigan at Portman Road in December. What an unbelievable atmosphere our supporters generated that night.

As we headed towards the festive period, another new face joined us in the shape of Darren Currie. He was a great lad and the first player Joe spent money on, with the rest being free transfers and loanees (what a brilliant wheeler-dealer manager he was). We had a very settled midfield at that time but Darren gave us fresh options. His set-pieces and crosses were second to none and he had all the skills and ability a player could wish for – a bit of a show-boater if you like. The only problem, clearly, was his lack of pace. Sometimes it seemed like he had a fridge on his back! He was so slow and, on reflection, I guess that's why he never played at the highest level.

I have to say that some of the treatment he got from our fans was a bit rough. Some supporters gave him stick but they seemed to overlook the fact he caused a lot of problems for the opposition with his balls into the box. He could provide great deliveries with both his right and left feet, but the boo-boys were just waiting for him to do something wrong. They were ready to pounce and, from a player's perspective, I have to say that's very unfair. If a player isn't working hard enough, fans have every right to criticise. That, for me, is acceptable because a footballer should always give absolutely everything to the cause. If they've got the best of intentions but are still getting jeered, though, then it just chips away at their confidence and saps enthusiasm. It can be very destructive.

Despite those problems, Darren made an unbelievable start to life at Ipswich by scoring on his debut at Queens Park Rangers. The only bad thing for him that day was that he wasn't able to join the rest of us for our Christmas party in Dublin. We were going straight from the ground to Stansted,

"One of the traditions at the club is that new players (or youth-teamers who make their debut) have to stand up and give a rendition of a song (I was very fortunate and missed out because I'd joined the club just after that season's Christmas party. I'm also the worst singer in the world so maybe it was my team-mates who had a lucky escape, rather than me)."

then hopping over to Ireland. He couldn't come because he still had things to sort out and finalise in terms of moving and getting settled in Ipswich.

Joe was fine with us going to Ireland. He gave us his blessing, but said the best possible tonic to send us on our way would be three points at Loftus Road. He warned us that a defeat would dampen the whole mood and, of course, he was spot on. It was a great incentive from a wily manager and it obviously paid off, because we won 4-2. We were actually 2-1 down at half-time but Darren came on just before the hour-mark and scored, followed by a fourth goal from Shefki. He and Tommy Miller were room-mates at the time and I know they'd been watching Soccer AM at the hotel in the morning. One of the features they did on the programme back then was the 'easy' celebration – big, exaggerated over-head claps. Tommy and Shefki both started doing it then, as did our fans behind the goal, and I think we were the first in the country to follow the new Soccer AM trend. For several weeks afterwards, all you saw on Match of the Day and The Championship was teams celebrating in that way.

As you can imagine, the dressing room was buzzing afterwards and I remember Joe said

Joker in the pack - Kevin Horlock was one of my funniest team-mates ever. He had us in stitches!

Hot stuff - Darren Currie celebrates with Darren Bent after scoring on his Town debut at Loftus Road.

Making his feelings known - Joe gets animated.

we'd made him very proud, which in itself was a great feeling. He said to enjoy ourselves in Ireland, behave and that he'd see us all back for training on Tuesday morning. What better way to kick-start our weekend. The only pity is that we were minus our new goal hero Darren, because with his outgoing and fun-loving personality, I know he would have had a whale of a time – just like the rest of us. We had a couple of nights out there, with the second being fancy dress (I went as a pimp!). On the first evening, as soon as we arrived, I remember the aim was to get unpacked and changed as quickly as possible – then meet in the hotel reception. We were having the time of our lives, laughing, dancing and singing (I remember we were all chanting '2-1 down, 4-2 up, Ipswich Town are going up').

One of the traditions at the club is that new players (or youth-teamers who make their debut) have to stand up and give a rendition of a song (I was very fortunate and missed out because I'd joined the club just after that season's Christmas party. I'm also the worst singer in the world so maybe it was my team-mates who had a lucky escape, rather than me). It's safe to say some are better than others. Some of the shyer lads do it with great reluctance because they've got no choice – they grit their teeth and get through it, because they know they'll be forced to otherwise. Others stand up and milk the attention, absolutely loving their turn in the spotlight (like Jason, who had no problem belting out American Pie).

Socially, that trip was one of my favourites. The atmosphere was brilliant and everyone was buzzing. We had a few drinks, as you'd expect, but I can honestly say everyone behaved in the right and responsible manner. That's not me trying to protect anyone – we all knew what was and wasn't acceptable and we knew we had a duty to Ipswich Town. Players get criticised for going away and having Christmas parties (the current team experienced that a few months ago) but – as you'd expect – I totally disagree. Of course, if things go wrong or get out of hand then it's not good. However, if everyone's responsible and just letting their hair down, enjoying their team-mates' company, then I think it can only be a good thing for morale. That was definitely the case in Dublin. We were doing really well in the league, the players got on fantastically and the spirit was unbelievable – no great surprise when your team-mates include jokers like Jim, Kelvin and Kevin.

As for the football, one of the highlights of the New Year was a 6-0 demolition of Nottingham Forest at Portman Road. We were on fire at the time and, although we still conceded a few, the belief was that we were always capable of outscoring our opponents. Our philosophy was that as long as we did that we'd be fine. We were encouraged to play

full english

open, attacking football and, of course, we were indebted to some wonderful contributions, mainly from the prolific Benty and Shefki. They were our equivalent of, say, Wigan's Nathan Ellington and Jason Roberts. We also scored a lot of goals from midfield. Tommy Miller, for instance, regularly chipped in and it was such a healthy situation to be in because goals were raining in from everywhere.

We hung in there right until the end and the automatic promotion spots became a three-way fight between ourselves, Sunderland and Wigan (as soon as we got back in the dressing room after our game we wanted to know how the other two had got on). All three of us had momentum and were riding on the crest of a wave at the same time. Sunderland were the eventual champions, but on the final day we could just about scrape second spot if Wigan drew or lost and we won at Brighton. For me, that game was one big headache as I suffered concussion after a nasty clash of heads with one of their players. I was still out there when Shefki gave us an early lead and, with raw emotion pumping through our veins, we momentarily thought we had one foot in the Premier League. Then things quickly went downhill.

Adam Virgo equalised soon after and then I had to go off with the head injury after about 40 minutes. I remember lying on the pitch, feeling really dizzy and nauseous, but was determined to play on – much to the consternation of our physiotherapist, Dave Williams. For a few seconds, we were having quite an argument. He was insisting I went off and I was adamant I could play on. I told him to work his magic and put a bandage on it, but he said it was a big, gaping wound and no bandage would be enough to stop the bleeding. It was only when I tried to stand up that I realised he was right. As soon as I attempted to clamber up on to my feet I felt sick and dizzy and had to drop back down to the ground.

I had to have stitches and I vaguely remember all the boys coming in at half-time and asking me if I was OK. By that time, Juliette was with me – not that I remember too much – and apparently I mumbled something along the lines of 'how are Wigan getting on?' (they beat Reading 3-1). The build-up and sense of anticipation had been huge, but the players knew from the crowd reaction that things weren't going our way and we were back to the lottery of the play-offs – and once again up against West Ham.

The good thing, or so we thought, was that we were another year older and wiser. We felt confident and knew what to expect in terms of the hostile Upton Park crowd. Joe had repeatedly warned and reminded us and we were all totally up for it. The bad thing, with the benefit of hindsight, was the psychological damage caused by that disappointment down in Brighton. We'd finished the season on a low ebb. Suffice to say, we made just about the worst start possible and were 2-0 down within 15 minutes. Drissa, I have to say, had one of his most forgettable games and was torn to shreds by Matthew Etherington, so it was no surprise to see him replaced by Martijn. I'd started as left-back but then moved over to the right. West Ham goalkeeper Jimmy Walker put through his own net from Tommy Miller's shot to give us a lifeline and then, incredibly, Shefki scored another priceless goal to make it 2-2. After the game we felt delighted. From the depths of despair, we'd finished with a draw and felt sure it was going to be our year. How wrong we were. The less said about the return game the better. We never got going and just seemed to be far too nervous. We were so close to getting through to the final but, when it came to the crunch, were left wanting again and never managed to move through the gears. Understandably, the crowd got on our backs. The atmosphere became

A kick in the teeth - Steve McCall and Dave Williams
help me off the pitch after suffering an injury at Brighton.

flat and subdued and, although we were still level at half-time, we weren't playing well. Joe told us as much in no uncertain terms and said we had to step it up a gear, but for whatever reasons we flopped. It was so disappointing, because we thought we'd done the hard part by getting a draw at Upton Park. I must say, though, that I was probably more devastated by the Brighton outcome than losing to West Ham. The feeling of being so close to automatic promotion, then being kicked in the teeth on the last day, left me feeling so despondent and maybe it was the same for some of the other lads. I'm not making excuses but I do feel we were mentally scarred by the whole experience. It was hardly ideal preparation for two draining play-off games.

Despite another disappointment, Joe still did a wonderful job that year. He was typically canny and used all his years of experience to make some very sensible and astute signings. He also helped, guided and acted as a father figure to a lot of emerging young players – stars in the making who are now very established in the current set-up, like Owen Garvan and Danny Haynes. Others, like Benty and Ian Westlake, made a name for themselves and, as a senior, more experienced player, I always saw it as my job to try and help them and guide them through.

Those boys were all so shy when they broke into the first team. They sat in the corner of the dressing room and barely said a word. Physically, they lacked muscle – almost as though they weren't fully grown – but thanks to a lot of hard work and dedication they emerged from their shells, built themselves up and became very strong. For me, having watched them develop and on some occasions almost coached them through games, it was immensely satisfying to see them progress as they did. One year they were cleaning our boots, the next they were alongside us in the first team. They were full of respect and enthusiasm and, for me, their emergence was one of the highlights of the season.

As it was, due to our play-off defeat and financial circumstances, the youngsters played an even bigger part the following year. The club badly needed to have been promoted and our failure meant that in order to balance the books some of the top players had to be sold. Tommy and Kelvin went to Sunderland, Shefki to Blackburn and Benty to Charlton. I was very aware that another era was coming to an end and, naturally, I was sad and disappointed to see our top stars depart. Off the pitch, we were losing some cracking lads and on it we were bidding farewell to a top goalkeeper who was our rock, an excellent goal-scoring midfielder and a couple of strikers who, between them, had plundered nearly 50 goals. To say that collectively they left a huge gap would be an understatement, as we were to find out to our cost the following year.

full english

the end of an era

It was always going to be a struggle after losing such a vast array of talent. Hardly surprising, then, that we missed those players so much during the 2005-06 season. The team found it hard to adapt, the new faces failed to make as much impact as we'd hoped and, generally speaking, we were inconsistent from start to finish. We finished exactly where we deserved – mid-table.

Bidding farewell to the departing lads had been hard to swallow, partly because they were among our top players and partly because they'd become good friends – not to mention big and important personalities in the dressing room. The flip side was that their exit paved the way for others to join and, in terms of finding another goal-scorer, Joe tried to compensate for the loss of Shefki and Benty by signing Nicky Forster and Sam Parkin. Both were proven scorers and Nicky, in particular, always enjoyed great success against us – including a hat-trick, I seem to remember, for Reading at the Madejski Stadium.

Off the pitch, he was another incredibly loud, confident character (probably the noisiest player I've ever come across). In the same mould as lads like Kelvin and Kevin, he was a constant joker – definitely the type of person you heard before you saw. He had the cheekiest, immature sense of humour but had us in fits of laughter, just like a naughty schoolboy. Football-wise, though, his move never really worked out. He never got going after being plagued by injuries and that, I know, was a massive source of frustration for all of us, not least him and Joe.

As for Sam, it was a similar story. I don't think he'll recollect his time with us too fondly and, for whatever reason, he too got a lot of stick from some of our fans. In fact, he was a bit intimidated by

it all and that's why his best performances – not to mention goals – came away from Portman Road. In training he was fine, sharp and prolific. But as soon as he crossed the white line for a match, especially at home, he became a completely different player – almost as though he was scared to do anything wrong. I knew how good he could have been. He should have been an excellent player for us but, sadly, the fans never saw him get close to fulfilling his rich potential.

Unfortunately, Nicky and Sam weren't the answer to our scoring dilemma and Joe kept trying different things. Adam Proudlock was one example, joining in January. He'd been at Sheffield Wednesday but upset his boss there by turning up late for training not once, not twice but three times. He kept oversleeping and was desperate for a fresh start with us, but again it never really worked out.

Like Adam, Gavin Williams also joined us just after Christmas. I think most people are already aware that he was a huge joker, although in the early days he was actually quite quiet and reserved. He'd pipe up with the odd funny comment, though, and at times I wasn't sure if he was being sarcastic or serious. As time went on and he became more comfortable in his surroundings, Gavin really changed. Far from being quiet, he was the life and soul of every party. He was constantly doing daft things like tying peoples' trouser legs together and on one occasion near the end of his time with us he got hold of a player's mobile phone (I won't name him to avoid embarrassment). He used it to send messages to the player's mum, announcing he was gay, and also to the manager (Jim), saying he loved him and begging him to play him every week. It was all pretty infantile but funny and harmless.

Gavin was another who fitted the 'naughty schoolboy' type and he was always a nightmare when he was out injured. When the rest of us were out training, there was always a concern that he was in the changing room meddling with our belongings. I found him a good laugh but he was one of those people you either loved or loathed. Some found him very entertaining, others found him irritating.

By making signings on a very limited budget, Joe, to his credit, was doing everything he could to try and replace the likes of Tommy, Shefki and Benty. Kelvin was also an impossible act to follow (he'd been in the PFA Championship team of the year the previous season, so that showed what a star he'd been). We had two young keepers on the books, Lewis Price and Shane Supple, but neither of them could fill the gap. Both were very young and still learning the game. They didn't have the experience or authority we needed and you can't blame them for that. They just weren't ready for the job.

Another new arrival that summer was to become one of my best friends and favourite team-mates – Sito. What a great guy. He was so funny, warm and loveable and the way he spoke – limited English with a strong Spanish accent – was pure comedy. In his early days I'd watch him have conversations with people and see him nod his head as if he understood. Then, as soon as their back was turned, he'd ask me what on earth they'd been going on about. Sito must rank as one of my most popular team-mates, too. I can honestly say no one had a bad word to say about him and rightly so, because he didn't have a malicious bone in his body. When he first arrived he was one big (or should I say little) mass of excitement, enthusiasm and determination but he soon found out that if he was to be a success at the club he had to find a level of form and consistency.

Sito is actually the star of one of my favourite-ever Ipswich stories and he gave us the best laugh when the players went out for that year's Christmas party. Footballers love a prank and he found himself at the centre of one when a few of us (I think Ian Westlake started it) told him the players were all wearing fancy dress that night, with the theme being superheroes. In reality, we would all just be in suits, with the real theme being James Bond. Some of the boys had special flyers printed, which they put up in the dressing room, and it was all very convincing. Had I not been in the know, I would have fallen for it, too.

The rest of us were there first, chatting and having a drink, when Sito burst in, making a spectacular entrance in a brilliant Batman costume (being so small, he would have made a better Robin!). To say the rest of us laughed would be an understatement. We were creased up but, to be fair, he took it in great heart. In fact, he stayed in his costume for quite a while before nipping home to get changed. As I mentioned before, new players had to sing a song at the Christmas party and, when it was Sito's turn to grab the microphone, he belted out some incredibly cheerful, catchy Spanish tune. None of us had ever heard it before but it was so uplifting we all found ourselves clapping and cheering him on. What a great sport he was and, largely thanks to him, what a fantastic night we had.

full english

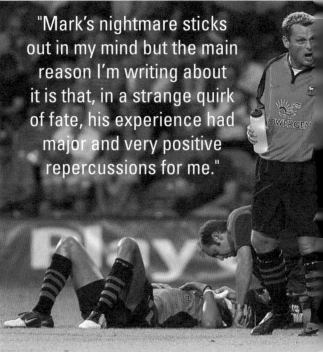

"Mark's nightmare sticks out in my mind but the main reason I'm writing about it is that, in a strange quirk of fate, his experience had major and very positive repercussions for me."

Talking of that year's sing-a-long, we were all given quite a surprise – and a real treat – when one of our other new boys, Vemund Brekke Skard, took his turn in the spotlight. Unbeknown to us, he actually had the most amazing, powerful operatic voice. Again, I had no idea what the song was. It was something Norwegian, I think, and we were all blown away. We were absolutely gobsmacked, and it's hard to believe one person could have so many strings to their bow – he was a professional footballer, a teacher, a qualified ski instructor and now, as we found out, a brilliant operatic singer (the same could not be said of Gavin, who had to sing despite the fact he was only on loan at the time. He couldn't think of anything so ended up murdering the West Ham anthem I'm Forever Blowing Bubbles. Jim had to chase him off the stage!)

Football-wise, Vemund was incredibly strong and fit but he wasn't skilful enough. He compensated for it to some extent, in terms of his phenomenal work-rate, but I think it's fair to say he wasn't the most talented of players. He certainly helped our party go with a swing, though, and from what I remember we had a double dose of festive celebrations that day. It was the players' party in the afternoon, followed by the club's do in the evening. Juliette was due to join me for the latter (she was one of the very few players' wives to be there and qualified for an invite because she taught Pilates to some of the Ipswich employees). However, after a few drinks with my team-mates, I have to say that I was in a bad way by the end of the afternoon. I phoned her and remember saying 'these boys are evil – they're trying to kill me!'. In fact, I could barely walk but I knew I had to sober up fast because a lot of important officials – including the chairman and directors – would be at the club event in the evening. We all had to be on our best behaviour.

Thankfully, it was alright on the night, so to speak, and I remember it was during the evening when we found out Jim planned to retire. David Sheepshanks made a special announcement

New lease of life – Mark Fish's unfortunate baptism of fire at Loftus Road gave me the opportunity to prove myself as a centre-half. I'm sure the conversion helped prolong my career as it was a role I performed both at Town and Grays.

but things got a little out of hand when Darren Currie jumped up on the stage and grabbed the microphone (Jim was supposed to speak next but found himself upstaged). Still a little worse for wear, he paid a glowing – if slurred – tribute to our team-mate, saying what a great guy he was and how much we were all going to miss him. He's probably quite embarrassed when he looks back on it now.

On the football front, Jason De Vos missed out at the start of the campaign, having suffered a nasty injury during our first game against Cardiff City, and in a bid to solve the problem Joe turned to a loanee in the shape of the highly experienced Mark Fish. He joined up with us the day before our match at Queens Park Rangers and I shared a room with him. My gut instinct on the signing was very positive. He was a big, powerful centre-half with a top reputation, having played for Bolton and South Africa. In fact, he was a huge star back home, almost his country's version of David Beckham. At face value, it seemed like another very smart

business move and, personality-wise, I liked him a lot, too. I'd met him a few weeks previously, towards the end of the previous season, when Hermann (then at Charlton) hosted a party in London. It was a very plush affair as he'd hired a big mansion set in beautiful grounds, which included a lake. Very posh indeed! All the Charlton boys were there but I was the only Ipswich player. Myself and Mark got talking and he struck me as a very nice guy, very laid back and chilled out.

Now, a few weeks on, we found ourselves as team-mates – but not for long, as fate would have it. We went on to lose the game at QPR 2-1, with Mark starting in one of the centre-half positions alongside Richard Naylor. However, I have to be brutally honest and say he had one of the most horrendous debuts I've ever witnessed. In fact, he only lasted until half-time before being hauled off – and that was it for his Ipswich career, just 45 minutes. I felt so sorry for him. Poor Mark just wasn't the player I knew from Charlton. He was carrying weight and so slow. We could easily have been three or four goals down, rather than 'just' two, and he was involved in errors for all of those chances.

Mark's nightmare sticks out in my mind but the main reason I'm writing about it is that, in a strange quirk of fate, his experience had major and very positive repercussions for me. Matt Richards came on in his place and, for the first time in my career, I moved from the full-back position to centre-half, alongside Richard Naylor. It was a pivotal moment and something I hugely enjoyed – and as everyone knows it was a position I went on to establish myself in during the rest of my time at Ipswich. My first time there went very well and it seemed very natural. I stepped in with ease and, in

full english

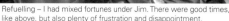
Refuelling – I had mixed fortunes under Jim. There were good times, like above, but also plenty of frustration and disappointment.

My Spanish amigo and I taking a breather..

the second half, I'm glad to say we became much stronger and resolute. As for Mark, his Ipswich career was over before it had begun. In fact, two days later – having freely admitted he'd had a stinker and concerned about his lack of mobility – he announced his retirement. It was hardly the best way for such a proven and successful player to bow out. I reckon he still has nightmares about those 45 minutes even now.

From my own point of view, though, I was very grateful. I hate to say it but Mark's horrific experiences at Loftus Road ended up giving me a whole new lease of life. It probably even helped me extend my career, because I've just spent the last season playing as a centre-half at Grays. As a full-back, where I'd always played previously, there was a very heavy emphasis on getting forward. You needed bundles of pace and energy and, as your career ticks on, it becomes harder and harder to produce those qualities. As a centre-half, though, the required attributes are so much different. Take a look at Jason – definitely one of the very best defenders I played alongside at Ipswich. He wasn't quick but he was so strong and intelligent – he read the game like a book and intercepted so much danger. I tried to do the same and managed to quickly adapt to my new position, so I've got an awful lot to thank Mark Fish for! I suppose I felt playing there also gave me a chance to put my football knowledge to use. I was 35, going on 36, and my motto as a centre-half became 'if you can't be quick, be smart'.

I was able to use my vast experience to read the game and, as the matches rolled on, I learnt more and more about being a centre-half. I realised that positioning and communication was everything and really enjoyed the challenge of something new. Two games stick in my mind. One was a 2-1 success at Millwall, after which Joe really praised me in his press conference. Bam Bam had been sent-off and, if I say so myself, I really had to defend well – more or less dealing with the situation on my own – to protect our lead. That was a great morale-booster but then, two days later, I was brought crashing down to earth as we lost 4-0 at home to Preston. It was a horrible experience and the less said the better. David Nugent murdered us, not least me, and I suppose in many ways those very contrasting results summed up our season so far – inconsistent.

I had one other real low in the game against Cardiff, at the end of November, when I was sent off for an alleged professional foul after just 13 minutes. I was furious with the decision and, after the game, confronted Cameron Jerome, who I felt had gone down too quickly and conned the referee. The pair of us were discussing it when who should walk past but my future team-mate (and then Cardiff striker) Alan Lee. He jokingly told me Jerome always goes down too easily in training, which made me feel even worse.

It wasn't the first time I'd met Alan. Our paths had crossed in the corresponding game the previous year and I've never had so much banter with an opponent in my whole career. Physically, we'd niggled each other and he was in my ear, questioning me and my technique, the whole game, especially when it came to corners because I was marking him. 'You're the worst defender I've ever come across', he kept saying. 'You're never going to win. You're rubbish'. 'I've seen bad players but you're the worst'. It was unbelievable and non-stop. Fair play to him, though. We won 3-1 and, afterwards, he came up to me and said well done. A younger player might have been bothered or put off, but I was too experienced for his tricks – it was water off a duck's back and just made me more determined. I always enjoyed my battles with Alan. His style of play really suited me, whereas I always struggled against certain other strikers, like David Nugent.

As for other games which stick out, who could forget our wonderful victory at Carrow Road. That was undoubtedly one of the highlights of the whole season. It was my first game back at Norwich, after the storm which had followed my comments two seasons previously. People were screaming abuse at me from the minute we pulled up at the ground. I was public enemy number one and the club even put a bit in the programme, reminding people what I'd said, which I thought was a bit irresponsible. There I was trying to forget about it and move on but there was fat chance of that if people were being reminded. Norwich went in front and all I could hear was their fans singing 'Wilnis, what's the score?' I didn't like it, obviously, but I expected it so it didn't faze me or put me off. It just made me more determined for us to get back in the game and we duly did that thanks to Jimmy Juan. Then, two minutes from time, we got our winner courtesy of Danny Haynes' famous 'Hand of God' goal.

How I celebrated. It was such a huge relief and I remember jumping and dancing in front of our ecstatic fans. I was so happy and can remember them singing 'Fabian Wilnis is a blue – he hates Norwich'. To be honest, I felt a little uncomfortable about that, too, because I didn't like being the centre of attention. A big part of me wanted them to move on to another chant, although I was obviously much happier to hear that one than the Norwich version. It was an unforgettable experience and all I can say is that I'm happy our coach was able to pick us up right outside the dressing rooms. I didn't fancy the prospect of walking through their fans much. This time I got straight on without doing any interviews, too. I'd had my fingers burnt from the previous occasion and learnt my lesson.

full english

Our inconsistent form and mid-table finish spelt the end of the road for Joe. He left us that summer but could definitely hold his head high. Our financial constraints, and therefore the need to sell top players, had crippled him. He'd had no money to spend and all his signings that year had been free transfers (apart from Sam, who joined for a nominal fee). There were lots of loanees, like Gavin, Adam, Jimmy, Mark, Ricardo Fuller (I wish we could have signed him permanently but couldn't afford him at the time) and Jay McEveley (who loved to moan so much about everything. He had the best job in the world as a professional footballer but never seemed to appreciate it).

Joe couldn't get the players he wanted and, in many ways, he was constantly working with one arm tied behind his back. It was no surprise, therefore, that we finished 15th. That just wasn't good enough and, for lots of reasons, it was a season to forget. Having said that, I was still very surprised and bitterly disappointed to see Joe leave.

The club sent everyone a text message during the close season, saying that unfortunately they felt it was best to make a change and that he was leaving by mutual consent. They said they wanted to tell everyone now, rather than wait for the news to break in the local media. I phoned Joe when I heard the news to wish him all the best for the future. It was such a shame to see him go.

Amid all of that disappointment, though, the very strange irony was that for me personally it was a memorable season. I maintained a level of consistency and, to my eternal gratitude, was voted fans' player of the year. To this day, I'm still very proud of that. I'd been told I was in the running and then one day, when Juliette and myself were having lunch in a restaurant, I got a phone call from Steve Pearce (now the club's press manager). He told me he had some good news for me and announced I'd won the award. In the end I think it was between me, Jason and Bam Bam – all defenders. I received it on the pitch before our last home game of the season, against Derby County, and it was one of the most special moments of my Ipswich career. Although I was pictured with my silverware before the game, I actually officially received it at a supporters' do that evening. In addition to the trophy, I was also lucky enough to be given a beautiful, engraved glass bowl, which still has pride of place on my fireplace.

I'd been fortunate enough to win the award at my previous clubs so knew what a great honour it was. I'd been happy with my form and consistency, as both a centre-half (a position I felt like I'd been playing in for years) and a right-back. However, to have it recognised and acknowledged by the most important people – the fans – was wonderful. It was confirmation I'd done a decent job during a difficult season.

Jim takes the reins

I was on holiday in Tunisia when news broke of our new manager – and I couldn't believe it when I discovered his identity. I got a text from a friend, asking me to guess who my next boss was. When he said it was Jim, I didn't think he was being serious. I thought it was all a big joke. I sent a text message to another friend, asking if there was any news on the managerial front, and he too replied Jim. Finally starting to believe the news, I sent a text to the man himself saying well done, wishing him all the best and making some early requests for lots of days off and a big pay rise! I added that I was looking forward to seeing him again after our summer break.

It was strange timing because a few weeks previously myself, Juliette, Jim and his wife had been out for a meal and we'd discussed the future. Having just retired from playing and been given such a heartfelt send-off from the fans, he admitted he was very keen to get into coaching. At the time there was talk of him preferring a move somewhere back in the North-West. A few short weeks later and he'd landed not just any old position but the top job at Ipswich Town. The meal had been intended as a bit of a farewell. We'd worked together for seven years, having arrived at more or less the same time and stayed in the same hotel when we first came to Ipswich. We'd been more than just colleagues. We lived very near each other and our families had become close, to the point that my girls and his boys were in a lot of the same classes at school and were always playing together. I was sad to see him go and kept wondering how I'd feel in that position, if I'd just hung up my boots and was about to step into the unknown, not sure where my next job opportunity would lie.

To be perfectly honest, I was surprised by the appointment. I always thought the board would go for a proven, more experienced manager, so he must have done a fantastic job to convince the board of his suitability. I believe there were some decent names on the short-list so full credit to Jim. He excelled in his interviews and, although the first year was always destined to be a steep learning curve, I knew he was determined to repay the board for taking a gamble. Initially, I was gobsmacked but when the news sunk in I was actually very pleased. At least, I was pleased for Jim. He was a good friend so I knew our relationship could make things tricky between us. He'd been my team-mate for so long and it's hard to go from colleague to boss. Like I say, I was happy for him but had good reason to harbour those fears.

The first few weeks after reporting back for pre-season were very weird, to say the least. To see

> " To be perfectly honest, I was surprised by the appointment. I always thought the board would go for a proven, more experienced manager, so he must have done a fantastic job to convince the board of his suitability."

full english

Clenched fist - Jim shows his emotion.

Always putting in 101%, against Norwich this time.

Celebrating with new signing Alex Bruce.

him standing there addressing the players – rather than being alongside us listening to someone else – was quite bizarre. At least it was strange for me. The others might not have found it quite so odd, but given our history I think it's fair to say I had the most trouble accepting and adjusting to the way things now were. For the first three months, I found it very difficult to call him 'gaffer'. To me, he was still just Jim.

It must have been surreal for him, too. We'd been through so much together as players and there was a real history, but now we found ourselves having to effectively take that sentiment away. I had to see him as my new boss, while he had to judge people on their football ability and pick the best players for his team – not do any favours for old friends. Some people accused Jim of doing that while he was manager, given his background with people like, say, Richard Naylor and Tommy Miller. However, I can safely say he's well and truly above doing anything of the sort and far too strong-minded and professional. Jim would only ever pick who he considers his best players and that's obviously the way it should be. I certainly didn't want or expect any favours, anyway. Far from it. I wanted to earn my place on merit.

Jim was quick to make his first new signings. He moved for Alex Bruce (everyone used to call him Steve, after his dad. He didn't find it very funny but, in jest, we kept on doing it anyway, just to annoy him), Dan Harding and Sylvain Legwinski (who was later crowned player of the year, despite missing the last few weeks with a metatarsal injury). Sylvain became a particular favourite of mine and we're still close friends. He was another senior pro but was also highly intelligent and a deep thinker. He became my room-mate and snooker rival, as we played against each other all the time. Sylvain's someone I've got a lot of respect for and I've stayed at his house in Fulham a couple of times, after nights out in London. Juliette and I also went to St Tropez with him and his wife, Madeline.

Unfortunately, we didn't make the best of starts to the new season. In fact, we lost our first three games, against Crystal Palace, Wolves and Leicester. Then, thank goodness, we registered our first point against Hull and that was followed by a brilliant win at Queens Park Rangers. For so many reasons, it was a massive result and a real milestone for Jim. It eased some of the early pressure on his shoulders and the fact the game was being screened live on television meant so many of our fans were able to watch and share the sense of occasion.

Bam Bam's big day - Richard Naylor receives a standing ovation as he and his children walk out on to the Portman Road pitch.

"I was absolutely gutted because testimonials don't come along often – especially in this day and age. I still had a very enjoyable day, though, catching up with my old pals and reminiscing about the success we'd shared."

On a personal note, I made a solid enough start. I was a regular throughout August but then picked up an injury the day before Bam Bam's testimonial (being staged on a free international weekend). His big match was against the Wembley 2000 team and I was so looking forward to seeing some of my old team-mates. As I was still a current player and therefore qualified for both teams, I was due to play a half for each of them. It was destined to be a really special day and something I'd been looking forward to for ages. Then, the day before, I was sprinting forward in training and felt something go. I saw Dave Williams, our physiotherapist, and he delivered the bad news. "It doesn't look good, Fab," he said, at which point my heart sank. I'd over-stretched my hamstring and was ruled out of playing any part the following day.

I was absolutely gutted because testimonials don't come along often – especially in this day and age. I still had a very enjoyable day, though, catching up with my old pals and reminiscing about the success we'd shared. In fact, it was a day I'll always cherish and in the evening we had a meal together at the Copdock Hotel. Bam Bam thoroughly deserved such a special and memorable occasion, having given such loyal and dedicated service to the club, and the fact we'd just won our first league game made everyone even happier. It certainly helped things go with a swing and I know it was a big monkey off Jim's back.

As a player, Jim was always very loud and vocal. As a manager, he was both of those times ten. He had a lot to get used to in a short space of time. In your playing days, you only really have to worry about yourself – your fitness, your performances, your position in the team. As boss, though, he had to worry about everyone and everything and that's a huge responsibility, especially with 25,000 supporters looking over your shoulder. Nevertheless, he appeared to be coping well. Jim relished the challenge and was definitely finding his feet, although it was frustrating for him not being able to influence things when his players crossed the white line. When he was out there with us he was constantly talking, cajoling and leading by example. Now, no matter how much work and preparation we did during the week, it must have been strange for him being stuck by the dug out. When the first whistle blew it was down to his players – they would either make him proud or let him down.

Due to my hamstring injury, I only managed one appearance in September, against Coventry.

full english

Jim swooped for a couple of new loan signings around that time, Mark Noble and Simon Walton, who were young guys with lively personalities, and one game that sticks in my mind from the early part of the season was our match down the road at Colchester United. To be honest, I remember it for all the wrong reasons as it was the first time Jim not only left me out of the team but out of his 16. I remember watching the game as a very disappointed spectator from the packed Layer Road stands. For Colchester, it was a huge game – arguably their biggest of the season – against their big brother from up the A12. They were having a wonderful season, as the surprise package of the Championship. Karl Duguid scored their deserved winning goal and that compounded my sense of frustration at not being out there to help.

Another game that stands out – although again for negative reasons – was our 5-1 home massacre by a Kevin Phillips-inspired West Brom. I failed to make the cut again but by now I was kind of prepared. Jim had never made promises to any of his players. I didn't expect him to because a manager can't make guarantees – too many things can happen like injuries, a loss of form or new signings. However, I was more determined than ever and duly, thanks to a lot of hard work, managed to win my place back as a regular starter throughout October. I remember playing Preston, Southend (when Lewis Price got injured after eight or nine minutes) and Luton, when we beat them 5-0 at Portman Road. That was a strange day because one of their players, Sol Davis, had a stroke on the way to the ground, which must have been very upsetting for the others to see. They still wanted to play – as I would in those circumstances – but struggled to concentrate. Their focus had slipped and, given

everything that had happened, it detracted from the quality of our win. It was developing into a real up and down season, for the team and myself. With a lot of new players on board and a rookie manager who wanted to try new things, there was a real experimental feel and I don't think we as a team or me as a player ever built up any momentum. There was no head of steam and, from my perspective, given my age and lack of chances in the team, I was starting to seriously think about my future. Not that anyone else would have known it, unless they knew me really well. I've always been a fighter and pride myself on my professionalism, especially as a senior player when it was down to me to lead by example. Whatever failings I may have as a player or person, I'd like to think any of the managers in my career would testify to my attitude. Even if and when I've not been in the team, I've always tried to support the other lads and stay positive, rather than moping or sulking. However, that's not to say I didn't get frustrated if I wasn't playing and this was one of those times.

One thing that really appealed to me was becoming a personal trainer, or possibly getting into the massage side of things, as it's something I've always found so beneficial. I looked into both, with a view to getting some work experience or doing a course, and was also very interested in doing some PR work for Ipswich. I wondered whether I might be able to attend a few meetings with potential sponsors, to use my background as a first-team player to make an impact and effectively help the club sell their brand.

I got some very encouraging feedback. The club were keen, open and helpful and got me involved in promotional situations like the one I've just described – almost using me in an

Left: Getting ready for the new season ahead.

Right: Jim beginning to feel the real pressure of management.

ambassadorial role. It was all very interesting food for thought, although I found it strange because being a professional footballer had been my life. Now, for the first time in years, I was having to consider a bit of a career change, albeit still connected to sport. Nevertheless, for the time being at least, I still considered myself a very determined and hungry player within the current first-team squad – and I made that clear when I spoke to people about my options. There was no way I was giving up just yet, just doing the sensible thing and looking ahead.

It was going to be such a battle, though, and my chances were dented to some extent by the arrival of David Wright - another full-back - in January. Jim also made three other signings at the start of the year – Jon Walters, Gary Roberts and the madman that is George O'Callaghan. As I've said previously, I've always had a soft spot for Irish people and George was no exception, especially as he had such a wonderful, zany sense of humour. He also does a lot of impressions, including an uncanny one of Jim (although Jim didn't find it very

funny!). One day on the way home from a game he grabbed the microphone at the front of the coach and launched into an amazing mickey-take of the boss. It was hilarious and, in terms of laughs, he'd definitely rank up there alongside comedians like Kelvin and Kevin.

My first taste of action in 2007 was in the FA Cup replay against Chester City. I hadn't been picked for the first match, but was chosen as right-back for the second and found myself up against Walters. What a player he was. I can't remember many more energetic, busy displays. He kept going and going, chased everything and certainly wasn't someone who gave up easily. My specific job was to mark him for corners but he was so hard to play against, because his movement and touch was so impressive. It was no wonder that Jim decided to snap him up on the strength of those cup ties and bring him to Portman Road. He must rank as one of the best – if not the best – Magilton signing. Thankfully, we managed to set the record straight with a 3-2 win against Colchester in January. I was

full english

Giving my all – although my opportunities were few and far between this season,
I always tried my hardest in the hope of holding down a place in the team.

an unused sub again, which was frustrating, but as a group we really wanted to do well for our fans, to show them that the first derby result had been a one-off slip-up.

From my point of view, my inactivity on the bench summed things up – I was there or thereabouts, but just couldn't pin down a regular starting spot. I did get a chance in our match at Stoke, though, which we managed to draw 0-0 – despite having what must be the smallest back four in the history of the Championship (ironic given that Joe Royle had previously referred to the Britannia Stadium as the Land of the Giants). There was me, David Wright, Sito and Dan Harding, up against towering, muscular strikers like Mamady Sidibe and Ricardo Fuller. To get a point in those circumstances was a real achievement and together we managed to ride the storm, being so pleased and proud that we kept a clean sheet.

February was a miserable month both for the team and me. We lost all four of our matches – and I didn't play in any of them. However, things definitely picked up again from the middle of March. I played regularly from then until the end, while the team only lost once in nine games, against Sheffield Wednesday. There was also a very special moment for me in the final match, against Cardiff, when I was captain and Jada and Kaylee were the Town mascots. What a wonderful family occasion that was.

Team-wise, our form had come too late but at least it offered hope and encouragement for the following season. For me, although I'd had plenty of disappointment throughout the campaign, I felt proud that I'd kept going. I never moaned or complained and hopefully I proved to Jim that I was still a useful person to have around, for my capability as a player when needed but also for my positive mental attitude. From my perspective, I must confess I was also very driven and motivated by the thought of a testimonial. Even when I felt down, that kept me going. I was so close to reaching ten years with the club and, if I'm honest, felt I deserved it.

Looking back at the season, you could say I was frustrated but also positive. That probably sounds like a real contradiction but it's true. Yes, I was frustrated because of my limited opportunities but I still felt relatively upbeat. There was no doom and gloom, like I'd experienced

Showing my appreciation –
here I am saluting the fans.

under Burley. This time, I still felt involved, rather than frozen out. I'd got used to the idea of a new manager and I respected him and his decisions. From his point of view, mistakes were inevitable in his first year but I knew how passionate he was and I knew he was desperate to succeed – just like I was. I enjoyed being part of Jim's experience, too, and all the time I was thinking how would I deal with things if I were manager? Would I deal with situations involving the supporters or the media in the same way? Sometimes I could see his point but on other occasions I couldn't. That's not to say he was right and I was wrong, or the other way round. Everyone handles things differently but for me, knowing the manager as I did and being at a similar stage of my career, it was very interesting watching and observing.

For me personally, I'm not sure I would have wanted to go from being an Ipswich player to Ipswich manager. I don't know how well I would have handled such a big and quick transition and would rather start out as an assistant and work my way up. Jim was straight in at the deep end and it was very much a sink or swim scenario. He deserves credit for the way he tackled and rose to the challenge. People can say what they like about him but one thing's for sure – he's got a blue heart. He was so passionate about the club and wanted them to do well, move forward and get promoted. For that I applaud him.

Jim was also a very hard worker. He clocked some long hours during that first year and got better and better in terms of his attention to detail, tactics and team talks. He learnt so much on the job, too, like when to make substitutions, how to make changes to improve the team and how to get a positive response. All in all, it was a steep learning curve for everyone and no disgrace to finish 14th. It was a respectable, mid-table position, with the promise of much better to come the following year.

Two other non-football related incidents stick in my mind from the 2006-07 season. The first – the far, far more serious and upsetting – concerned the murders of five Ipswich prostitutes, just before Christmas. You may wonder why I'm mentioning it in a book like this but for me, as an Ipswich Town player, an Ipswich resident and a human being, it was a deeply troubling

full english

and upsetting time. Needless to say, the players decided to cancel their annual party that year, as a mark of respect for the victims and their families. No one individual made that suggestion. They didn't have to, because everyone felt the same. It wouldn't have been right or appropriate to celebrate during such a dark time for the area. Ipswich is such a quiet, peaceful town and to find it at the centre of the world media spotlight was surreal to say the least.

You could feel the tension everywhere. Everyone was very cautious, looking over their shoulder and people – especially women – didn't dare venture out on their own. The police were everywhere and I certainly felt very protective of the girls in my life. I never wanted Juliette to go out on her own, especially after dark, and always wanted to know where she was going and when she'd be back. Members of my family back home were too scared to come over from Holland and people were phoning all the time to check we were OK. That may sound like an over-reaction but it's understandable to worry about your loved ones when you're sitting at home watching this nightmare unfold on TV. It was a very dark period in the history of Ipswich and also Ipswich Town, given that these girls had worked and been murdered so close to Portman Road. The news coverage kept showing the ground and that just brought the horror even closer to home. It was a very poignant time for me and every day I was taking calls from friends, family and even the Dutch media. The whole affair had such an impact on everyone.

The other situation I wanted to mention, which is absolutely incidental in comparison, was the ill-fated, unauthorised trip some of the players made to Amsterdam, the day after our 1-0 victory against Birmingham on New Year's Day. There were seven of them in total – Alan Lee, Chris Casement, Gary Roberts, Scott Barron, Gavin Williams, Daryl Knights and Billy Clarke. I was actually with some of them on the first night, having been given a couple of days off to go back to Holland after the New Year. At the time I wasn't really involved in the team, so the club had granted me a bit of time off. I'd heard the others talking about their trip and honestly just assumed it had been cleared by the boss. It was only when I got home – and experienced the storm - that I realised what they'd done.

Everything had been fine to start with. It was only me, Alan and Chris because the others had missed their flight to Amsterdam. They had to get a later one to Rotterdam, then travel down by train or taxi. Jim was absolutely furious with the players in question and, I have to say, had every right. It was totally inappropriate, especially so soon after the murders, and they should have been resting anyway. It was hardly the smartest move, five days before the next game, and it was bad and very disappointing publicity for the club. The seven in question were named and shamed and boy were they made to suffer – having to run and run and run during training. The rest of the lads were playing five-a-sides but those seven were made to keep on running, under the watchful eye of Jim and Simon Thadani. They looked shattered – like it was the end of their first day of pre-season training – but for the rest of us it was quite amusing to look over and watch them struggling.

Poor Jim. As if he didn't have enough to contend with in his first year. Still, he may not have thought it at the time but I dare say having to deal with incidents like that helped him learn and develop as a rookie boss. He probably emerged from it all as a better and more experienced manager because of it.

all good things must come to an end

I didn't realise it at the time but the 2007/08 season was to be my last as an Ipswich player. There were only two months during the whole campaign when I was really in the thick of things – October and December – and the rest of the time I was resigned to a bit-part role, playing my last ever game against Portsmouth in the FA Cup in January. I'd started off in a positive frame of mind and it had been nice to welcome back two friendly, familiar faces during the summer – Pablo Counago and Tommy Miller.

End of the road – the clock was ticking down on my Ipswich career.

Pablo and myself had become great friends during his first spell with the club and we'd kept in touch. I'd previously been out to his home in northern Spain and then during his time in Malaga I went back out to see him and his girlfriend, Lara. Pablo was playing that weekend and myself and Lara sat there in his house listening to the game (not that I could understand much of the commentary) and then waited for him to come home. Malaga lost 5-0 and after each of the goals Lara was groaning and saying she didn't think he'd be in a very good mood.

The original plan had been to go and have a night on the town but wisely, after such a heavy defeat, he decided that might not be appropriate. Instead, we found a quiet little restaurant and swapped all our news over a nice meal. Pablo's a lovely guy, very warm and friendly, and he and Sito became good friends during his second stint at Portman Road. It was understandable, given that they were fellow countrymen, and it reminded me of my relationship with Martijn.

Tommy was also a very welcome addition to our squad, both as a player and person, because he's such a fun and outgoing guy, and Jim also moved to solve our goalkeeping dilemma by signing Neil Alexander. When he got into his rhythm, he was top-class and saved us so many times – particularly with a few penalty stops. However, when the chance came to move home and join his boyhood heroes Rangers, it was far too good an opportunity and, although I

full english

Here I am seeing red after a two-footed
lunge on future Town player David Norris.

One of the best – Jason De Vos was a top de
He was so intelligent and read the game like

was sorry to see him go, no one would have denied
him his dream move back to Scotland.

From a personal perspective, my season got
off to the worst possible start after being sent off on
my first appearance, down in Plymouth (I'd been an
unused sub for the first two games). What made it
even more frustrating was that the same thing had
happened against the same opposition the season
before (bizarrely, I'd also been red-carded against
the Pilgrims in a home game in 2004) – and on
both occasions the referee in question was Kevin
Friend. The previous year, in the October, I'd been
given my marching orders for two bookings. This
time, I'd only just stepped off the bench in place
of Alex Bruce – yet just four minutes later I was
trudging back to the dressing rooms.

I remember the incident clearly. I failed to
control a pass – I think from memory it bounced
awkwardly off my foot – and in a desperate bid to
win the ball back I'd stretched and made a very rash
tackle. Had it been a great challenge I'd have been
singing my own praises, so I have to take the rough
with the smooth and admit that this wasn't my finest

piece of footwork. My tackle was effectively a two-
footed lunge and the player on the receiving end
was none other than future Ipswich player David
Norris. Funnily enough, he came over to me when
he signed for us and started taking the mickey out
of me. Up until that point, I had no idea it was the
same player. I didn't have any complaints about the
referee's decision that day (although he's not exactly
on my Christmas card list). All I can say is that I so
desperately wanted to get the ball – perhaps I tried
a little too hard.

Jim was cross with me and rightly so. I
was disappointed in myself, too, because I knew
it was an irresponsible move from such a senior,
experienced player. To be sent off twice in two years
by the same referee against the same opposition
was uncanny. And the fact it was against Plymouth
at Home Park made it even worse – I had around
seven hours during the coach journey home to
stew and reflect on my stupidity. The whole thing
circled round and round in my mind. It was torture
and the kind of thing that could only happen to
me. I was suspended for three games and, with

Skipper for the day – here I am leading the team out for our FA Cup duel with Portsmouth. We would have won, were it not for the heroics of Pompey goalkeeper David James.

an international break thrown in for good measure, it meant I wouldn't be able to play any first-team football for well over a month, from mid-August until early October. That, looking back, was the beginning of the end. The writing was on the wall.

Jim, to be fair, gave me one new outlet by asking me to get involved and help out with the reserve and academy sides. That was great, but I was still determined to play. It was a tough time, though. I only played one game in November and the rest of the time I wasn't even getting on the bench. Then I came on for Alex in our match against Bristol City in December and that sparked a mini revival. Typical me. There was never a dull moment as the roller coaster of my career started one last upward climb.

Things were going well again until Jim decided to put me back on the bench for our home game against West Brom, which we won 2-0. I thought 'here we go again', but then he made me skipper for the cup tie against Portsmouth. What an honour that was. We were desperately unlucky to lose the game. Liam Trotter was very harshly

sent off early on and then David James made some outstanding saves to deny Danny Haynes. Had they had any other goalkeeper between the posts, we'd have definitely won the game. Even Hermann Hreidarsson, then playing for Pompey, admitted that afterwards when we swapped shirts.

It was so disappointing, but overall things still looked bright. I'd just skippered the team in a really gutsy, battling performance and felt I played well. I was still in great shape and never thought for one second it would be my last official appearance in a Town shirt. After all, if the likes of Teddy Sheringham, Dean Windass and Gary Speed (all great examples and sources of motivation to me) could continue playing to such ripe old ages, why couldn't I do the same for Ipswich? In some way, looking back, it's a small crumb of consolation that my final game was against Premier League opposition. However, to say I was anything other than sad and disappointed would be a lie to mask my true feelings.

I have to be brutally honest about the way things changed for me in general after that game, too. I was made to train with the reserves and

My ball – here I am in typically combative mood against Dion Dublin.

academy boys, rather than the first team, and it wasn't long before I had a big fall-out with Jim. I was just so frustrated. I still felt I could do a job, but he told me to consider my age and the other players who could play in my position. I was so angry and disillusioned at what I heard and the whole thing developed into a very heated confrontation, which was a pity because it might have been avoided if we'd spoken sooner. I would have preferred it if he'd pulled me to one side at the start of the season, explained the situation, told me I wasn't part of his plans and perhaps asked me to help out with the academy boys. I would have listened and, although I might not have agreed, I'd have slowly and reluctantly accepted it. Instead, I carried on until the new year with a false hope that I might play again – and was made to train with the young boys without any explanation. That was what really bugged me, because I felt I was being treated like an outcast.

Our argument took place in full view of everyone, by the side of the training pitch, and it's a good job they were there, especially Jason De Vos and Alan Lee. They told me to calm down. They said what a good example I'd always been and not to ruin it now by doing something rash and stupid. They told me to see the bigger picture and accept my situation.

They were right, but I've always been a fighter (not physically, of course, but in terms of my place in the team). To have to come to terms with the fact there was no point fighting anymore, that I had no chance or hope, was incredibly difficult. My emotions were all over the place and that was a big reason why we clashed. I'm ashamed to say that I reacted badly by kicking a ball at Jim. Thankfully, it missed him by a foot or so but taking such drastic action shows how upset I was. People who know me will tell you how very out of character that was. In games there are times when you might get worked up but generally speaking, in everyday life, I hardly ever lose my temper. I'm very easy going, rational and controlled. I'd always tried to be a positive influence and I can't stand it when people are moody and sulky – that just sucks energy out of others around them. No wonder the players looked so shocked to see me that irate. It felt horrible afterwards, too. I remember phoning Juliette before I left the training ground and I was literally shaking. Knowing me as she does, she was more shocked than anyone to hear that I'd let myself go like that.

A day or two later, when the dust had settled and we'd both had a chance to cool down, I went to the manager's office to apologise. I said I shouldn't have over-reacted and we ended up having a very good and positive chat – just like the old Fabian and Jim. It was a very constructive meeting and, by the end of it, everything was fine. He praised me for my attitude and the honest truth is that I should have shown more respect to him and he should have shown more respect to me. It works both ways. We spoke about everything and he explained how he saw my role in the squad – essentially being there to help develop the young lads – and I suppose what's sad is that it took an argument to get us talking like that. Still, at least things were out in the open now. We'd cleared the air and put our cards on the table. I felt strangely relieved because finally I knew where I stood. Now it was time to move on and I dare say we both learnt from the experience. I certainly feel that if, one day, I become a manager I'll make a point of being up front with my senior players, especially those who aren't part of my plans. In the long run, it's best to be honest.

As I slowly and reluctantly came to terms with my situation, knowing I was going to be released at the end of the season, I have to say I lost interest in the remaining games. When I look at the results now, barely any of them register in my memory but obviously I know the lads finished eighth – just one agonising point outside the play-offs. My new brief, and therefore main focus, was helping the young lads, who I was still training with every day. I really did enjoy it, too, especially when I knew what the situation was in terms of playing. I could focus my energy on trying to help the others, rather than hoping and waiting for a chance. However, at the back of my mind, almost secretly, I clung to the thought that at some point I might make one last appearance – albeit just five minutes or so – to say a proper goodbye to the fans. It never came, though, and so the supporters' last memory of me in competitive action was during that cup game against Pompey (although I was an unused substitute for the next league game, a 1-1 draw against Stoke).

People have asked me whether I ever considered going out on loan but the easy answer is no. I was never interested, partly because of my age but mainly because of my family commitments back in Ipswich. Going on loan is ideal for a young player who is desperate to prove himself, climb the ladder and get some first-team football under his belt. It's something I'd certainly recommend, but at that stage of my career I didn't fancy living out of a suitcase again.

I did, however, get a chance to bid my farewells after our last home game of the season, against Hull. Myself, Sylvain and Jason (who had also decided to retire and was moving back to Canada) led the team on their lap of honour and I suddenly knew how Jim had felt, when he'd done exactly the same thing two years previously. It was emotional to say the least. I had my girls with me and the other players gave us a guard of honour, which was a fabulous show of respect. It was a job to compose myself and I had goose bumps as I slowly navigated my way round the pitch. The tears were welling in my eyes and I really didn't want it to end. It was probably a good thing the girls were there, because they were chatting to me and, to some

full english

extent, providing a bit of a distraction – otherwise the fans might have seen me blub.

I have to thank those supporters. To get a reaction like that was overwhelming and I'm so thankful, because I'll always treasure those memories. They looked after me and supported me for nearly ten years, never once booing me or getting on my back. I had a great relationship with them and hopefully they liked and respected me both as a player and a person, as someone who gave their all and loved the club. Richard Naylor made a nice speech in the dressing room and they gave the three of us (Jason, Sylvain and myself) a signed shirt and beautiful Mont Blanc pen.

Town staged their end-of-season awards night that evening and I was very fortunate to receive a special memento, in front of a packed audience of 350 people at Trinity Park. Not that I saw it coming. I honestly didn't have a clue. You know what it's like at awards dos, where you've seen and applauded so many presentations during the course of the evening that you're beginning to get a bit restless. Well, that's what happened to me. Jim was speaking and I suddenly 'zoned in' when I realised he was describing someone. He was talking about a player who had been with the club a long time, someone positive who always tried their hardest and was a true professional. When the penny dropped and I realised he was talking about me I couldn't believe it. I quickly slipped my dinner jacket on, straightened my wonky tie and went up to receive a very beautiful glass award. It was engraved with the words 'Fabian Wilnis – the ultimate professional'. Again, it was overwhelming and the response I received from everyone was so genuine and heart warming. I got the biggest cheer of the night.

Talking of Jim, I have to say he was the person who led the way in terms of convincing the board and owner Marcus Evans that I deserved a testimonial. At the end of the previous season, I'd been at the club for nine and a half years. Jim was the one who made it possible and I can still remember the day he called me over to his office at the training ground. He said to sit down and then gave me the best news I could ever imagine – that the club would be granting me a testimonial for my service and loyalty. All I had to do was officially put down in writing my request, asking permission for a match to take place. Jim didn't have to do what he did but knew how much it meant to me. I was over the moon and remember giving him a big hug.

A few years ago there was a Reading player, Graeme Murty, who had also been at the club for ten years. He too asked for a testimonial but the Royals chairman, John Madejski, said no because footballers earn enough money (although he later relented). I don't believe it's about the money, though – it's about recognition and appreciation from club to player. Just look at people like Roy Keane, Ryan Giggs, Ole Gunner Solskjaer and Alan Shearer. They all had a testimonial but do you think they did it for the money? I don't think so. There's a part of me that's still coming to terms with the fact I'm no longer an Ipswich Town footballer. I still walk round the ground now, seeing the same familiar and friendly faces, and it feels so natural. It was my life for nearly ten years, after all, and in many ways the club became my second home. I've been asked how I'd like to be remembered by the fans and that's simple – as someone who was always professional, gave his all and as someone who was Ipswich through and through. To be held in such high regard would make me very happy and proud.

from blues to grays

The summer that followed was a strange one as I had no idea what the future held. I'd done my FA UEFA B licence course straight after the season at Keele University in Stoke. It's a fast-track course for professional footballers who have been in the game for at least five years. John McGreal and Paulo Wanchope were among the ten ex-players there. It's intensive, starting at 9am until 7pm (or sometimes later). You get so much knowledge from the course but it was very exhausting. What other people learn in a year we had to do in 12 days.

Before now, I'd always been an integral part of Ipswich Town. I had a nice break, then a close season and then everything was geared towards making a positive start to the new campaign. Now, having been released, I found myself stepping into the unknown as I had no idea where my career was heading. The only thing I knew for certain was that I wanted to carry on playing. As everyone says, you're a long time retired and it was important to me to stay in shape for my testimonial (more of which in the next chapter). The last thing I wanted was to run out in front of all those people feeling unfit and out of shape, with everyone saying 'look how much weight he's put on!'.

My big hope was to find a club locally because I didn't want to leave Ipswich. It was very much my home town now and I had no intention of moving. The most obvious option was Colchester United and I heard lots of whispers throughout the summer. First they were interested, then they weren't and then they were again. Unfortunately, though, I never heard anything official from the club so that option was closed. Then, randomly, I got an offer from a club in Scotland but that didn't exactly fit into my criteria of staying local, so was a complete non-starter.

"Now, having been released, I found myself stepping into the unknown as I had no idea where my career was heading. The only thing I knew for certain was that I wanted to carry on playing."

There was also a fair bit of interest from local non-league sides and I trained a few times with Needham Market. I enjoyed my time with them and it was a good way of staying fit. Their chairman used to be in charge of Ipswich Wanderers and he knew Juliette as she taught the players Pilates, so that was how it initially came about. I was also very impressed with their manager, Danny Laws.

Needham had done really well the year before, finishing runners-up in the Ridgeons League premier division, and were full of ambition. I liked what I saw and they offered me a job to become Danny's assistant. I even took a few of the training sessions which I enjoyed, although I think some of the players were a bit shocked by how hard I worked them on the weight side of things, with the push-ups and abs exercises. They weren't really used to it and, even at the age of 37, I was leading the way in most of the running exercises. As a professional, I'd been used to keeping in tip-top shape because it was my job, but for these boys playing

full english

New surroundings - here I am getting early tastes of the action with my new club, under the watchful eye of our manager/chairman/owner Mick Woodward.

was more of a hobby and they all had day jobs on top of their football.

As news of my availability spread, I received a few calls from other non-league clubs wondering if I fancied joining them and I trained twice and played one game for Bury Town. I felt a real connection with Needham, though, and, after being involved in several training sessions, was due to play a match for them against Diss. However, while stretching in the warm-up, I picked up an injury which meant I never actually got to play a game for them.

Around the same time, Grays Athletic had been in touch. I didn't know much about them but a quick check on the Internet revealed that they were only an hour or so away, which I could live with. They played at a decent standard, too, and after a few phone calls I ended up driving down to play in a friendly against Gillingham. It went really well and, without wishing to be disrespectful, I could really see the difference between a Blue Square Premier side and one from the Ridgeons League. I was still keen to play at the highest level possible and so it was after that game that I made a decision – I wanted to sign for Grays. Needham had been great to me but I just felt that playing at their level would have been too much of a backward step, having just come out of the Championship.

Grays beat Gillingham 2-1 and after the game I had a chat with manager/chairman/owner Mick Woodward. Tim O'Shea was his coach and both of them said they would love me to join their club, to provide some experience and pass it on to the younger players in the squad. I was sold, although remember being quite firm in telling them I was still open to other offers. I had an injury at the time (and was destined to be sidelined for about a month) and said that if they wanted to sign me it would be fine. I also said they wouldn't have to pay me until I was fit again and ready to start playing. They seemed more than happy with that and so, with the paperwork sorted, the next eventful chapter of my career was about to begin.

Injury kept me out for the first few games but I finally made my debut against Salisbury, which we lost 1-0. It was odd because in the Gillingham friendly we'd passed the ball so well, but now the serious business was underway we were much more route one. That just seemed to be the way of the league, though, and I think I defended and dealt with more high balls in one season than I did in ten at Ipswich.

At Town, the emphasis had always been on keeping the ball down and passing it, so this was a culture shock. There was nothing wrong with

the boys' fitness. They were all in good shape and were physically prepared for the rigours of a tough division. What let them down was their decision making. Instead of looking up when they had the ball and having a decent overview of the pitch, they just kept looking down and that lack of vision, for me, was another very obvious difference. As a result, we played a very direct game and there was no flair in the team whatsoever.

In my second game, against Eastbourne (which we also lost 1-0), I went up for an aerial challenge and got a whack on the top of my head. The guy elbowed me and I needed seven stitches. Juliette took one look at me afterwards and couldn't believe it. There was blood everywhere and she said I wouldn't have any teeth left by the end of the season. It wasn't exactly the best of starts. We lost matches against Mansfield and Crawley and then Woodward resigned as manager following a 3-1 defeat at Woking. O'Shea took over and in his first game we won 2-1 at home to Wrexham. We played some really good football – our best of the season so far – and afterwards the mood was extremely upbeat.

However, the club were about to shock us when, just two days later, they told us they were bringing in a new manager. Poor old Tim only lasted

one game – which we won – and if he felt hard done by it was no wonder. I wish the board had been a bit more patient. I'm convinced that had they stuck with him, the club would have finished a lot higher in the table. As a boss and a coach, he certainly got my vote. He always looked to play football and his tactics were spot on.

Wayne Burnett, the former Plymouth player and Fisher Athletic boss, was unveiled as the new man in charge – our third manager in just two months. However, he really wasn't the answer to our problems and the team wasn't really playing well. We were relying on far too many long, hopeful balls forward and unfortunately things went from bad to worse. Every month, Wayne would bring in new strikers, either on loan or trial. In fact, over the course of the season, I think we must have had 20 to 25 front men. They'd usually come on a month's loan and be brilliant in the first couple of training sessions and then again on their debut. In the second match they'd be average and then in the third, fourth and fifth they'd go downhill. Then they'd disappear back to their parent club and the cycle would start all over again with different players. Each time, we all thought 'here we go again'.

Unfortunately for Wayne, he was gone by the end of the January. He hadn't really been able

full english

to improve the team and a lot of players came and went during his brief tenure. I wasn't used to that and for me it was incredible. Lads would come and go so the squad was constantly changing. I remember one guy, in particular, who was only with us for a little while and was a typical 'wide boy'. I didn't understand half the things he said and he kept calling everyone 'yo bruv'. It was like a whole new language to me. One day I had a fall-out with him because he kept farting around me in the gym. I said he should show some respect to the rest of us, but that was like showing a red rag to a bull. I got such a mouthful back and it soon became obvious he was spoiling for a fight. I was amazed. The other lads stepped in to stop things going that far and afterwards I got speaking to one of the more sensible boys in the dressing room. He told me not to take any notice and said that for some of these guys every day was a battle, because of the backgrounds they came from. They belonged to communities where confrontation, and in some cases guns and knives, were part and parcel of everyday life and being aggressive was their way of expressing themselves.

I later found out that the lad who squared up to me had spent a year in prison and the whole thing really got me thinking. It made me realise how lucky I was. I had a wonderful life both in the game and privately, with my family at home. However, for some of my new team-mates, football was the only good thing going for them. It was their outlet and when they weren't training or at games they were back in their communities, dealing with the grim reality of everyday life. It was impossible not to feel sorry for them.

Because of where I'd come from, there was always this recurring theme where they thought I was some loaded, multi-millionaire. The players would go on about the credit crunch not affecting the Wilnis household. To start with, I'd retort with lines like 'I wish'. After a while, though, I just gave up and played along. Whether there was any resentment or whether it was just banter I'm not entirely sure, but I always liked to think it was the latter. I never felt there was any real jealousy so could deal with it – even if it did wear thin after a while.

At the start of the season we were training in a local park. At the beginning of each session we had to push the goals into place, then at the end they had to be wheeled back into their storage space. We also had to chain them up, to stop people stealing them, but one day when we arrived the nets had been taken so we had to train with goals with no nets. It was like a different world to the cosy, luxurious world I'd left behind at Ipswich. Thankfully, it wasn't long before the club moved us into new training facilities at a sports academy in Loughton (a lot of top boxers use it, too). The

> "For some of these guys every day was a battle, because of the backgrounds they came from. They belonged to communities where confrontation, and in some cases guns and knives, were part and parcel of everyday life and being aggressive was their way of expressing themselves."

facilities there were great – to start with at least. After a while, the pitches became a bit bumpy – leading to a lot of muscle injuries - but at least there was a nice gym and canteen and, overall, it was a huge step up from the park. It did lead to a lot more jibes about my finances, though, as the place was directly opposite the Bank of England. Every day someone would refer to it as the Bank of Wilnis.

Talking of money, I got a bit of a shock one day when one of my team-mates phoned me wanting to borrow quite a lot of money. It was for a new car and he said he needed help because there was some kind of problem with his wages. After mulling it over, I said I couldn't help him because I had no guarantee he'd be able to pay me back. The player in question did his best to convince me, though, and I eventually lent him a big sum of it (Juliette has only just found out about this. She probably wouldn't have agreed with it if I'd told her). To his credit, my team-mate eventually paid me back, albeit in instalments. It was an odd situation for me because no one had ever asked me to lend them money before. At Ipswich, everyone was in the same boat. We were all earning a decent wage and could pay our way, but now it was different.

Obviously, the whole financial structure of the club was different to Ipswich. At one point things got serious when it was announced the players had to take a 50 percent pay cut. The mood and morale

> "Obviously, the whole financial structure of the club was different to Ipswich. At one point things got serious when it was announced the players had to take a 50 percent pay cut. The mood and morale in the squad took a nose-dive but, thankfully, the cut never happened."

in the squad took a nose-dive but, thankfully, the cut never happened. Something was sorted behind the scenes.

There were a few other things, though, in terms of differences between Town and Grays. At Ipswich, every player had a 'boot boy' who would be in charge of cleaning our boots after training and games. We'd give them some money at Christmas and at the end of the season. At Grays, though, it was a totally different story. The players were responsible for their own footwear (and washing their own kit). After a few goes at scrubbing my boots, I jokingly asked if any of the lads wanted to earn some extra money. I said I'd give them a fiver a week for cleaning my boots. One of the boys was interested but said he wanted £20. I said that was far too much, so we settled on £10. It was great – although the arrangement only lasted a couple of days because he then went out on loan. The whole thing was such a contrast to what I'd been used to. One other major difference was the situation with travelling to away games. As most Ipswich fans probably know, the team stay overnight before just about every match on the road. It was and still is par for the course and all part of the preparation. At Grays, though, it was the complete reverse – to the extent that we were originally going to travel on the day for a January match up in Barrow. For those of you who don't know where that is (I didn't have

full english

a clue!), it's way up north near Carlisle. To even consider travelling there on the day was almost farcical. However, the club were keen for us to do that because it would save a lot of money on a hotel.

Rather than being cramped on a coach, the plan was to travel by train – leaving King's Cross in London at 8am and then changing at Stoke. If everything went according to plan, we would then arrive at 1pm and walk from the station to the ground (which would have taken around 20 minutes). I couldn't believe my ears, not least because it would have only taken one of the lads to be late (which would inevitably have happened) for the whole thing to be thrown into chaos. We knew that if we didn't get the Stoke connection we wouldn't arrive in Barrow until 3.15pm – hardly ideal preparation for a 3pm kick-off! Eventually, with a lot of discussion and pleading all round, we went up on the Friday. That was very much the exception to the rule, though, and

we travelled all round the country for matches on the same day – even far-flung destinations like Torquay and Wrexham. In fact, I think we only stayed overnight twice, for the Barrow game and our FA Cup tie at Carlisle.

Wayne eventually departed as manager after a defeat against Burton on January 17th. Gary Phillips, who had been his assistant, took over which made sense as he knew the club and the players. However, in true soap opera style, after just four or five games, the club announced they were going to appoint someone else, the former Carlisle boss Roddy Collins. It was a bizarre situation as the new guy would have been my fifth manager of the season. Worse still, word reached us that he was a real disciplinarian who wanted the players in every day – even Sundays. I knew I needed to recover from my travelling to training every day and of course the matches. There was no way I could go along with that, to drive all the way in on my precious days off or on days when I might be back in Holland. Needless to say, the other boys felt exactly the same.

Gary's last game was against Altrincham on March 7th, which we won 2-1 (Collins watched on from the stands). It was one of our best performances of the season, packed with lots of passing and movement. I felt very positive and genuinely felt that in terms of matches and training we were making progress. Gary was improving us and I said as much in conversation with one of the directors. I wasn't really happy about the fact he was being replaced. After that game, I remember he gathered us all in a circle on the pitch and thanked us all for our help and effort during his brief spell in charge. That, I thought, was that. However, the following day, I got a phone call from Gary, saying the club had changed their mind and that he was going to stay on until the end of the season, as originally planned. I was delighted.

When I'd signed on the dotted line for Grays, I never expected to have the season I had. I never dreamt there would be such turmoil and so many ups and downs. It was a real eye opener. To be honest, there were lots of times during the season when I thought to myself 'what on earth am I doing here'. I'd be lying if I said differently and admitted as much to my team-mates during the season. They were great, though, and very reassuring. They told me not to give up and that they needed me, which made me feel that I didn't want to let them down.

I've got so many memories of my weird but wonderful season, like the time when we lost 4-1 at Histon – and were four-down after 30 minutes. It was a midweek game and our goalkeeper had suffered concussion on the Saturday. In fact, he was carried off on a stretcher after a nasty clash of heads. However, such was the injury situation at the club (our other keeper had a groin problem and could hardly walk, let alone kick a ball) that he was asked to play against Histon – and agreed. I told him he must be mad and could see during the warm-up that he wasn't right. He looked dazed, his eyes were all droopy and when I asked him if he was OK he said 'no'. However, it was a needs-must situation and credit to him for giving it a go. Others wouldn't have even contemplated it and I know that at Ipswich if a player suffers any kind of head injury they're out for two weeks at least.

> "When I'd signed on the dotted line for Grays, I never expected to have the season I had. I never dreamt there would be such turmoil and so many ups and downs. It was a real eye opener. To be honest, there were lots of times during the season when I thought to myself 'what on earth am I doing here."

We had three physiotherapists during the course of the season. The first was Dicky, then Andre and lastly the pretty 24-year-old Becky. The boys did love her, and I mean LOVE. Every day she got a proposal by a player to leave her boyfriend and marry him – which she always kindly rejected.

I've discussed a few negatives from my time with the club but I wouldn't want people to get the wrong impression. I'm only trying to highlight the contrast between life at Ipswich and life at Grays, between the Championship and the Blue Square Premier. I loved my season at the Recreation Ground. Something attracted me to them right from the start, even if people questioned my decision and thought I was mad. Juliette felt that sometimes. She thought I'd be better off playing more locally, or better still quitting altogether and moving with her and the girls back to Holland. Once I'd made the decision, though, I was never going to go back on it. I'm a fighter, not a quitter, and was always going to see the season out. I certainly haven't

full english

Hit with the boys - you can see why our physio Becky was so popular among the Grays players.
Right: I was so touched that so many Ipswich fans came to watch my last ever appearance in the professional game.

got any regrets. Far from it. I experienced so much in a short space of time – some good and some not so good – and met some great people along the way, the vast majority of whom were warm and welcoming from day one.

I've always followed my gut instinct and am a big believer that everything happens for a reason. I was so fortunate to lead the 'luxury' life at Ipswich. We had a lovely stadium and top-class training facilities and they were contributing factors to why I performed so well for them for so long. Everything is in place for the players to succeed there. You're given a chance and a platform - it's down to the individual to grab it and perform to the best of their ability.

At Grays, it was the opposite in terms of the aspects I've just described and I suppose I wanted to see how I'd cope at a lower level. It was that desire to carry on playing, based on my love of the game, which drove me on. I'd change some things, but other experiences I wouldn't swap for the world. I certainly wouldn't have traded my team-mates. They helped me and, in turn, I really hope I helped and educated them. They seemed to look up to me and give me respect, but I'm not a 'big-time' person and certainly never thought I was any better than any of them. I was just one of the lads and

we had some good times, both within the club and out on the town in London. Of course, there was always lots of banter and, as I said earlier, there was always a perception that I was rich. They'd often make jokes in terms of what they thought I had. All in all, I must have had 60 team-mates during the course of the season. The vast majority were great guys with a very different but entertaining sense of humour. At Ipswich, the players were focused and driven, because they played at a higher level and were more professional. At Grays, though, there were extra distractions and they probably didn't concentrate or take it as seriously as they should have done. That led to too many mistakes on the pitch but I understand why they approached the game as they did.

Some of these guys had tough lives, riddled with deep-rooted problems. Football was their outlet. If they applied themselves a bit better, though, I'm sure a few of them could carve out a career in the Football League. I joined Ipswich when I was 28, but most of the lads I'm talking about are 19, 20 or 21. Anything is possible and hopefully my background highlighted that for them, because it's all about taking football seriously and doing the right things, in terms of attitude, training, lifestyle and diet. It's never too late.

It was a big experience for me to play against teams I'd never even heard of, too. Nearly every week I had to go home and look up sides and destinations on the Internet – places like Barrow, Weymouth and Lewes (I thought the last one was spelt Lewis and named after someone!). In the Championship I got used to playing the same teams over and over again – Derby, Southampton, Stoke, Palace etc. This was a completely different ball game and I played in some very strange and unique environments. Some places I'd been to before, like Oxford and Rushden, but the vast majority of times it was a whole new experience and some of the away dressing rooms were about the same size as my garden shed.

I've also got great memories of our home stadium, the Recreation Ground. It's not exactly housed in the best of areas – sometimes I didn't like leaving my car there – but it certainly had a warmth and charm to it. It's right in the middle of a housing estate and it always amused me the way people would gather at their upstairs windows and balconies to watch our games. They had a better view than if they'd paid to get in. Juliette and the girls came to see one of our home matches, against Histon, just after Christmas. It was freezing and, if I'm honest, I think they were a bit surprised by

what they found, having been so used to the plush surroundings of Portman Road. I'm glad they saw it, though, and it meant a lot to me.

As for my own performance during the season, I don't think I ever reached the standards I managed for Ipswich. I made more mistakes than I used to and there were a few reasons for that. First of all the preparation – it's never ideal travelling for an hour before training and home matches over the course of all those months. Secondly, the conditions - the bumpy pitches, quality of the balls and pedigree of the players. If you're used to playing with footballers of a decent standard, they'll drag you to a certain level. However, if you're lining up with players whose standards are not so high, it's very easy to let things slip.

My family also moved back to Holland when the season started (we wanted Yasmin to start her secondary school education where we knew she wouldn't have to move part way through), so I missed having a routine at home. Whenever I had two days off in a row I flew back to Holland, which also meant I wasn't getting the rest I needed. I really missed having my family around and wanted to be with them as much as possible.

My last game in professional football was against Forest Green Rovers. The build up was special because I organised a coach and discounted tickets for Ipswich fans who wanted to come along and share the experience with me and so many of them turned up in support. The game itself felt different. Before kick-off, the players were coming over and asking how I felt about my last match. To be honest, I was OK. I had my usual routine, my normal rub, but this time I gave every player plus the coaching staff a bottle of wine as a thank you for the season, as a farewell gesture. The most

full english

Feeling the emotion - it really was the end of an era when the final whistle went in my final game. Thankfully, Juliette, the girls and so many supporters were there to support me.

important thing for me was that my family was there, supporting me from the very first day until the last.

The game was one to forget. We were trailing 1-0 at half-time but won 2-1. Just before the end (they don't have clocks at the ground) I asked the referee how long we still had to play. He told me ten minutes and that's when it really hit me. My last ten minutes as a professional footballer were about to start. I felt the emotions washing through me and those last few minutes were like a blur. I couldn't really focus or concentrate and, after the final whistle, my emotions took over. Nineteen years of professional football had gone. I just bent over and tears came flooding out of my eyes. All my team-mates came over and had a little word with me to say well done and, after I composed myself, I went to the fans to wave my final goodbye. I said a few words and expressed my thanks, then threw my shirt, boots, socks and shin pads into the crowd.

The Grays chapter of my career was life changing and an important part of my football journey. At Ipswich or a similar-sized professional club, the players don't realise how lucky they are. They grow up in an environment where it's normal to have everything done for them, like their kit washed and their boots cleaned. Now I was training in all kinds of weather conditions, on all kinds of

pitches, often with balls that looked more suited to rugby than football. We trained in a public park, with a goal that didn't have a net, and at times it seemed a million miles from the grand and impressive set-ups at Portman Road and the Ipswich training ground.

To experience the other side has made me realise just how lucky I was for all those years. I appreciate it so much and like to think that my experiences in the last year will stand me in good stead and benefit me if, one day, I become a coach. I've been at opposite ends of the football spectrum and the last year has been a real roller coaster ride.

a year I'll never forget

To say I was pleased, honoured and excited to be granted a testimonial by the club would be understatement of the year. The news was such a thrill and my mind was instantly buzzing with countless and varied ideas to make it as special as possible. My main priority, which has never changed, was to share and enjoy events with the fans and people of Ipswich.

My testimonial committee have worked to arrange things for everyone and, to that end, I have to pay huge credit to the tireless, unbelievable efforts of them all. Led by Juliette, they are Duncan Foster, Mark Lomas, Adrian Horne, Dennis Tennial, Keith Suffling, Steve Flory, Steve Hayward-Jones and Mike Cooper. There's no way the year would have been so successful, or run so smoothly, without their invaluable help and I thank them from the bottom of my heart.

I wanted my testimonial year to be something people would remember, something that would leave a lasting impression, and that's why the committee came up with such a mix of events, to cater for different tastes. My situation is slightly strange in that I'm no longer attached to the club. If you think of other testimonials, the player is generally always still on the books and the match is usually their swansong. For me, having already said my goodbyes, I felt it was very important to do as much as possible to promote the events and stay in the public eye. I've tried my hardest to remain in peoples' minds and the last thing I wanted was to disappear off the radar and then resurface just before the match itself. Basically, I didn't want anyone to forget about me!

The year started off with the launch of a calendar featuring yours truly, which was a big success and something I was incredibly pleased with. The idea was to use shots that highlighted the different aspects of my life and personality. Naturally, football was in there but so too were images of me with my family and friends and of me relaxing by doing things I love, like playing the piano and roller-skating. I wanted the pictures to reflect me as a person and the end product was something to be truly proud of.

The calendar was launched just before a fashion show, organised by the brilliant Pam Davis, which took place at the Seckford Theatre in Woodbridge. Again, it was a real success and for this one I was indebted to seven of my old team-mates – Danny Haynes, Dean Bowditch, David Wright, Tommy Miller, Richard Naylor, Pablo Counago and Pim Balkestein (plus a few wives and girlfriends). They were all great sports. I knew a few of them were quite nervous beforehand and understandably so, but they gave their all and got into the spirit of the night, which was great.

November and December were spent heavily promoting the calendar, which included lots of signing sessions in shops and supermarkets. I also handed lots out on a few hospital visits, which was something I found very fulfilling (as I always did as a player). To go on to a children's ward and make the little ones smile is a wonderful feeling.

At my request the testimonial committee donated £1,000 from the fund to the Ipswich Town Community Trust, which is such an incredibly good

full english

A few members of my fantastic FAB10 committee at the fashion show.

Everyone was dressed up beautifully at the 'Blue and White' FAB10 private party.

Magician Matt Edwards showing me a little trick under the watchful eyes of Dennis Tennial.

cause and was my way of giving something back to the club, people and town which has become my second home. I fully intend to make more donations in the future. People may not realise how much work they do, as is undoubtedly the case with so many other charities that approached me throughout the year. So many people are involved with so many good causes and it would have been easy to support more, but I decided to back the Community Trust. I hated saying no and hope people didn't think I was being disrespectful in turning them down, but wanted to put my heart and soul into one cause.

January was a quiet month and then in February the committee organised a private party at Keo Bar Bistro in Ipswich. It was an invite-only event and very glamorous. As guests arrived they walked along a red carpet and had their photo taken – making them feel like real celebrities – and there were one or two surprises when they were inside, too. They were treated to some top tricks from magician Matt Edwards and then danced the night away to the music of Irie J.

Everyone was brilliant and dressed accordingly in the blue and white Ipswich theme. I had such a brilliant night and it was the perfect way to really celebrate my testimonial year. Town's current first-team players were unable to attend because they were travelling back from Preston that day but among those in attendance were Alan Lee and Kieron Dyer. The then assistant manager John Gorman came along to show his support and so too did former Town hero Simon Milton.

The committee also arranged a special six-a-side football tournament, where people could form a team and then the one that got through to the final had a chance to take on a side made up of former Ipswich players (including me). Then, as things really gather momentum, comes the big day – my testimonial match against Colchester United and dinner on July 25th. It'll be so good to run out for one last appearance at Portman Road. Throughout last season, I stayed in touch with a lot of the Ipswich boys so still felt in the loop. I managed to see a few games and when suspension ruled me out of the Grays match with Burton, I was able to get along and sit with the Town fans for the FA Cup match at Chelsea.

I was also at Portman Road for the recent match with Norwich – a game that turned out to be Jim Magilton's last as Town boss. I was very surprised by the news of his sacking - and not least by the timing. The Norwich performance was one of the best I saw them produce all season. In front of a full house, the players showed passion, hunger and desire to get a positive result. They were doing it for the fans, the club and especially their manager, who had been under real pressure from some supporters and the media. After the high hopes at the start of the season, given the funds made available to strengthen the squad, the criteria was to get automatic promotion, or at least make the play-offs. It was always going to be tough for Jim, given those high expectations. Eventually, he paid a heavy price for not delivering what everyone had hoped for. The writing was on the wall, although I felt sure the club would wait until the end of the season and then make a decision.

I want to wish Jim all the best for the future and thank him for everything he did for the club in the ten years he was there – seven as a player and three as a manager. Although it's sad to see him go, I'm sure plenty of opportunities will unfold for him. His last three years at the club will stand him in good stead and it's been a real learning curve. If he's available and emotionally ready, I'd love to see him play in my testimonial, but I can understand it might be hard for him and too soon after his departure. We'll see - only time will tell. One thing's for sure - Ipswich definitely made world news in those crazy few days. First by appointing Simon Clegg as their new chief executive, followed by sacking Jim and then – the following day – making the sensational appointment of Roy Keane. Every national paper gave pages of coverage so instead of Ipswich being a sleepy little town in Suffolk, we were suddenly front and back page news. It gave the whole town a massive boost.

Town's last two results were brilliant, under Keane. They won their final games of the season - an impressive 3-0 victory at Cardiff followed by a 2-1 home win against Coventry. All in all, the fans finished on a high after what had been a disappointing, inconsistent few months. Supporters are talking about and looking forward to the new campaign, season tickets sales have surged and everyone is wondering what kind of players will be brought in during the summer. It's all very thrilling and I'm more excited than ever about my testimonial match on July 25th.

I had originally hoped the committee could get my boyhood heroes Feyenoord to Portman Road. They were the club I grew up supporting but the starting date for the Dutch season changed and that altered their plans. Playing Colchester will be great, though, and not least because it's a local derby. I really, really can't wait.

After that, it will be time to bid farewell to my life as a professional footballer. I don't think I'll ever say a permanent goodbye to Ipswich Town or the fans but on that day, at least, I'll have a chance to give them a wave and thank them for all their incredible support.

full english

juliette's story

They say that behind every good man is a good woman and that's certainly the case for me. Juliette is my best friend and soul-mate. She has been a rock throughout my entire football career, from my early days juggling playing commitments with studying to the highs of Ipswich Town and the Premier League. I wouldn't have wanted to share the experience with anyone else. It's been quite an adventure and, in a book about my football life, it seems only right and proper that she has a say, giving an inside view of being Mrs Wilnis.

"I hadn't grown up with football. In fact, I hated it when my dad used to watch it on television so when I started dating a footballer, I didn't really appreciate exactly what that would entail. I knew he had to train four times a week and in those days we used to just see each other after we'd finished college. I had my own social life and network of friends and because of that I didn't ask too many questions or take too much notice.

Then, a couple of years into our relationship, one of his friends told me I should go and watch him play, because he was actually very good. I gave it a go – Fabian's brother took me – and, while I enjoyed it, I found it all a bit overwhelming. Having not come from a football environment, or ever been into sport myself, I found it amazing how passionate and excited supporters and parents got. It was all a bit of shock! Why all the fuss about this silly game, I asked myself?

That was my first taste of live football and, while it might be a bit of an exaggeration to say I was hooked, I enjoyed it and was keen to see more. It makes me smile when I look back on those days - no one could accuse me of dating a footballer just for their money! Fabian was with NAC Breda back then and one of my strongest memories is of his ancient old Ford Escort, dating back from the 1970s. It guzzled so much petrol and back then his first contract – which was worth peanuts – more or less only covered his fuel costs.

We were both still studying, too, and after moving in together we soon discovered our newfound life of independence would be quite a struggle. Gone were the cosy, cushy days of living with our parents. Instead, it was a battle just to make ends meet. I was studying in Amsterdam, he was studying in The Hague, we were living in Rotterdam and Fabian's football team were in Breda. Anyone with any knowledge of Dutch geography will know that means a lot of travelling! I was 19 and I remember looking at the other NAC Breda WAGs, some of whom were in their early 30s, and thinking how old they were. It amuses me now, having reached that age, to think that some of the young girlfriends probably look at me and think the same thing.

One of my fondest memories of NAC Breda was when they got promoted to the Dutch Premier League. We partied all night. We didn't arrange a hotel and I had to drive back home. Fabian was completely drunk. I remember I lost one of my contact lenses and had to drive back with Fabian sitting next to me, unconscious because of the booze. It was the slowest drive ever. Fortunately, it was very early in the morning so there were hardly any cars on the road.

In 1995, Fab had moved on to De Graafschap when I fell pregnant. Our first daughter, Yasmin, was born there but I was in Rotterdam, visiting my parents and taking my mum to the airport to go to Surinam when I went into labour. It took us by surprise because she came four weeks early. I went to the toilet that morning and realised my waters had broken. Fabian had been on a night out in Nijmegen, very near the German border, where we lived when he moved to De Graafschap. He'd only had a couple of hours' sleep and then suddenly received a frantic phone call telling him to get to me as quickly as possible. It would have given him such a fright and he must have driven incredibly fast, because he managed a two and a half hour journey in about an hour and a half. As it was, we had to wait for the baby to come naturally and a night later she finally arrived. Fabian had two dreadful nights' sleep, because of his night out and being up with me, and then had to play a game at the weekend. It must have been hard for him but I know he was an extremely proud father after Yasmin arrived. He took a Polaroid picture in to show off his first little girl.

As wonderful as that time was, as any new parent will know, a little baby in the house means a complete lack of sleep and to say Fabian doesn't cope well when he hasn't had a full night's rest would be an understatement. It was difficult for him because of the nature of his job. Being a footballer obviously means being physically fit, sharp and alert, but I doubt he felt any of those things for the first few weeks. Around that time, his agent told him a club had shown some interest and that they were watching him – but he refused to identify the name of the side. However, Fabian didn't perform well – because of the sleep deprivation – and when we finally got the agent to reveal the mystery team he told us it was Ajax. Talk about lousy timing.

We learnt from that. We realised just how important it was for him to get his sleep, to help him excel with his football, and when Jada and Kaylee were tiny babies he slept in the guest room for three months. It made all the difference. I remember Martijn Reuser's girlfriend, Petra, saying how crazy I was to let him off the hook for three months. She would never do that when she and

It was so great to see the other wives again at Richard Naylor's Testimonial Dinner

Martijn had a baby. He could maybe have a night off the day before a match but the rest of the week he had to stay in their bedroom. When their baby arrived, Martijn begged to have some proper sleep and she finally gave in. It made Ragna Hreidarsson and I laugh, because we both knew what it was like to have a newborn baby and how it turns your life upside down.

Just as during our time in Breda, we also made some excellent friends where we lived in Doetinchem. That, for me, was our big move – bigger even than coming to Ipswich. I loved city life and was a Rotterdam girl. Doetinchem, in comparison, was so small and I must admit I felt homesick in the beginning. Looking back, though, I wouldn't change a thing and that experience paved the way – and prepared us both – for moving to England.

The huge irony, though, is that just before Ipswich made their offer myself and three girlfriends had come over for a short stay in London. It was my first ever trip to England. It was a very wet, grey and miserable day and, as our train sped up from Harwich to Liverpool Street, I can vividly remember saying 'this place is so depressing – who on earth would want to live here!' Little did I know that a month later, I'd be doing just that! My friends teased me for years about that and I was never able to forget what I'd said. Of course, with the benefit of hindsight, I didn't mean it. I love Ipswich and the same goes for Suffolk and England, but those early days here were stressful to say the least – and not just because of my negative first impressions.

One day at work it all got too much for me and I fainted. I had to be taken by ambulance to hospital and was told I'd had a miscarriage – without even knowing for sure I was pregnant. We'd been trying for another baby but I didn't want to do a pregnancy test on my own. Fabian was in England, while I was spending so much time travelling between the countries getting things sorted. It was hard for Fabian, because he could only comfort me by phone and felt really bad about that. We just wanted to be together but it wasn't possible. Between us, we just had to be strong and get on with it.

Fabian's such a family-orientated person and he was delighted when, in early April 1999, we were finally ready to move into our first house together in Ipswich. It felt great for the three of us to be together, although my situation was strange because about six months before I'd started a new job as a distributor for a health company. Not only did my training involve me going to Dallas, I also had to make monthly trips back home to Holland. Aside from that, though, we were happy and settling into our new life in England. The Ipswich WAGs were a warm, welcoming bunch and I soon made friends.

The people at the club were friendly and the team that got promoted was a team where friendship played a big part. I remember David and Alison Johnson, who made me feel at home

I was very proud to see Fab with Kaylee and Jada being mascots on the pitch

(especially because we both had a daughter of nearly the same age). Colette and Jim Magilton stayed in the same hotel and then we all moved to the same area. We understood each other very well. Their son was the same age as Yasmin, so we were all together in the same boat.

Having recovered from the disappointment of my miscarriage, we were still very keen to extend our family and try again for a second child. To be honest, there was a time when we questioned whether it would happen so we were both over the moon when I finally fell pregnant late in 1999. That meant I was seven months' gone – and therefore carrying around a huge belly – for the trip to Wembley in May 2000. What a day that was. I remember as we stepped up into the coach the club had arranged for us, everyone looked so smart. I didn't have a clue how big the day would become and just enjoyed the ride to Wembley. I was then gobsmacked when I saw the amount of people and the blue and red crowd. I've never been to Wembley before and didn't realise how big it was. I remember walking with my big belly (I felt I walked like a goose) to find my seat. It took a while before I found it and was really happy to finally sit down.

When the final whistle blew, it was party time. Fabian rang me from the bus and was drunk before it even got moving. I was so happy for him and couldn't believe the blue flags and banners as we drove up the A12. When we arrived in Ipswich, I saw Fabian at the Suffolk Showground. I was obviously pregnant and had Yasmin with me so couldn't really join in the celebrations but the atmosphere was fantastic. The day after it was great to see all the people waving at the team when we were in the Town Hall. So many supporters came and all I could feel was pride, for the team but especially of course for Fabian.

Our second daughter, Jada, was born during that summer, when Fabian was due to be on a pre-season trip with Ipswich. A huge argument had developed over the fact Fabian was made to go on the tour. Burley was adamant he should join the other players and kept ringing him every day leading up to it to check whether the baby had arrived. They were at loggerheads and Fabian dug his heels in because there was no way he was leaving me all on my own (our family and close friends were obviously back home in Holland). My contractions began just before they left and then I was told I was three centimetres dilated – the baby was coming. After a conversation between the club and our family doctor, the late Dr Lazar, he was finally allowed to stay. That, we thought, was the end of it and beautiful Jada was born on July 23, 2000.

full english

Then, within hours, Fabian got a phone call. It was Burley to say there was a flight booked in his name for 8am the next morning at Stansted. We were flabbergasted. Our daughter hadn't been in the world 24 hours and yet now he had to contemplate flying away from his family for (in my eyes) one meaningless friendly in Latvia. I'd been joined by some of our family by then and was so stressed by the whole situation I told him to go. From my perspective, I was very sad, angry and upset. I'd just gone through childbirth and my hormones were all over the place. The whole incident was incredibly traumatic and I couldn't believe he was forced to leave me when our baby wasn't even a day old.

The Premiership years meant Fabian's income went up and our lifestyle changed a bit. We were able to buy things without looking at the price tag. I enjoyed shopping at the PC Hooftstraat (the Dutch Bond Street) and we were able to go to posh restaurants. However, money is not a big issue to us. We never had any arguments about it, because we knew we were both quite sensible, although after a day of shopping I never dared to tell my mum what I bought or how much I spent. She would have had a heart attack, if she knew that what I'd spent in one day was equal to one or two months of her wages. We were fortunate to share the money with our family and friends. We paid for our parents to go to Indonesia and Surinam. We took our relatives to nice restaurants and were able to buy presents for our friends.

> "Then, within hours, Fabian got a phone call. It was Burley to say there was a flight booked in his name for 8am the next morning at Stansted. We were flabbergasted. Our daughter hadn't been in the world 24 hours and yet now he had to contemplate flying away from his family for (in my eyes) one meaningless friendly in Latvia.."

When Fabian scored against Manchester United I thought it was so unreal. It was the day before his 30th birthday and I managed to get Sir Alex Ferguson to sign his autobiography before the game. I framed his Wembley shirt and we celebrated the success with Martijn and Petra. Life was good, with a goal against Man U and a newborn baby. His 30s couldn't have started any better.

In December 2000, I went with our friends, Olaf Lindenbergh (who used to play for Ajax) and his girlfriend Claudia, to Old Trafford. I really wanted to see the stadium and we stayed in Manchester for two days. We went shopping at the Trafford Centre first and then the day after we went to watch the game. Jada was just five months old and Olaf carried her in a baby bag to the stadium. She had a red, woollen hat on that covered her ears and she slept through all the noise.

I was very excited and had tears in my eyes when I saw Fabian coming down the tunnel. I was so incredibly proud that he was playing at Manchester United. I couldn't believe that a year and a half earlier he'd been running out at De Graafschap and now here he was playing in the Premiership. I went to the players' lounge hoping to see Victoria Beckham, but she wasn't around. David was there with his boys and parents, though. It was quite unreal to be in their players' lounge and see top-class footballers. Their cars were driven in front of the lounge for them, so they could leave immediately – that didn't happen at Portman Road.

I wanted to see more Premiership stadiums but, because of the babies, it was hard to travel so far without family around. One day I went to Arsenal with Fabian (he was injured) and it was great to be in the players' lounge again to see these top players in surroundings other than out on the pitch. Thierry Henry, in particular, stood out to me. He was much taller than I thought and very handsome!

The first season in the Premiership was fantastic. Fabian suddenly became a high-profile player. The Dutch media was interested in him and there were even rumours about him playing for the Holland team. There is such a huge difference in terms of Premiership and Championship coverage. When you play in the Premiership, you're put on a pedestal. People adore you and sometimes I had to drag Fabian off that pedestal when he was at home. I didn't accept some kinds of behaviour and he respected it most of the time.

Just three months after Jada was born, I found out I was pregnant again with Kaylee. It had been our intention to have another baby very soon, but two in one year was quicker than either of us expected. After she was born, Fabian had similar problems with his sleep, even though he was sleeping in the guest room. It was down to us to find a solution to make the situation work and a little further down the road I got a break of sorts when Ipswich had their big match against Inter Milan. I went along and it was the first trip without having the babies in tow. As strange as that was, it was nice to be with the other wives again and – suffice to say in such an amazing city – we had a wonderful time. I particularly enjoyed the shopping because finally, after two years of pregnancy, I was able to buy nice clothes again. I immediately bought some high stilettos, because I was fed up of wearing flat shoes for two years.

Within six or seven months, I realised that I needed some help with the girls and that's when we were fortunate enough to meet our nanny, Claire. She was only 19 but became a big part of our lives for the next three and a half years. With her help and input, I was able to pursue my dream of becoming a Pilates teacher.

While things were happy and settled on the home front, Fabian was having a rough time at Ipswich. Burley wasn't playing him and that was a hard and frustrating period for both of us. People were surprised he wasn't being used, because they thought he could make a difference, and they were asking me what was going on. I didn't know what to say.

All I could do was be sympathetic and supportive to Fabian, just as any wife would. There were times when he came home so frustrated about how he was being treated and I'd tell him to keep everything indoors. He was allowed to vent it on me, but I didn't want other people to know about it. I had to keep him calm whenever he'd been treated unfairly. Other people can talk to their friends about problems at work but, because he was in the public eye, he couldn't say much. Fabian had times when he went out to party a lot, just to get rid of the frustration. For me, it wasn't easy because I was stuck at home with three children and no family or babysitters around.

Thankfully, though, those dark days under Burley's management were the exception to the rule. Joe Royle was a lovely man who always listened. Fab was really fond of him and so was I, having met him a few

full english

I was happy to join the girls again at the Inter Milan match

Petra and '7 month pregnant-me' celebrating the promotion at the Suffolk Showground

Visiting the Hreidarssons in Iceland

times, and I also liked Jim, having been good friends with him and Colette, during his days as an Ipswich player. We became close to the Magiltons and, in terms of friendships with other players and their partners, I'd say we went through different stages with different couples. Fabian and I were always the entertainers and loved having dinners and parties. One year, when for some reason Ipswich weren't playing on New Year's Day, we had a brilliant New Year's Eve party where I cooked dinner for several of the players and their wives (like Jim, Sito, Pablo and Jason De Vos). We also organised evenings where we'd have a game of Pictionary. It was so funny, especially when Sito or Pablo had to draw a word they didn't understand in English! It was great fun. I loved Sito and went to see him and his girlfriend Tanya in La Coruna, Spain. He could really make me laugh.

Petra, Martijn's girlfriend, had a fantastic sense of humour, Ragna Hreidarsson was every bit as crazy as Hermann and I was also close to Thomas Gaardsoe's girlfriend, Anne. The Premiership days remind me of those girls. We went to Iceland with Hermann and Ragna and it was funny to see that they are the Beckhams of Iceland. Ragna would often show me the Icelandic Hello magazine, which contained photos of them. We lived in the same street and I remember when I was heavily pregnant I wanted to go in their Jacuzzi, but Ragna was very doubtful. She was so happy she didn't let me do it, because my contractions started a few hours later. The thought of having a baby in her Jacuzzi! Ragna and myself went to Denmark to meet Thomas and Anne's families and to see their hometown. I remember Hermann suddenly called Ragna while we were there to say he thought he'd dislocated their little girl's shoulder. Ragna was stressing out but in the end everything was OK. Hermann just forgets how strong he is.

Players came and went and I became close friends with Lara (Pablo's other half) and Lalaicha Diallo, now the ex-wife of Drissa Diallo. On Fridays before away games they stayed over at our house and we always finished a few bottles of wine. I think Lalaicha will always associate me with rose wine. I went over to see her in Paris and we went to Vigo and Malaga to see Lara and Pablo. We had a great time together and went out to party a lot in Ipswich. It was great when they later came back to Ipswich.

In more recent years, I spent time with Dan Harding's wife Vicky (who used to call me Queen Bee, because I looked after the organisation of things and discussed with the club anything which mattered to the wives), Vicky Wright (David's wife) and Emma Currie (Darren's other half). Madeleine Legwinski also became a good friend of mine and we went to St Tropez with her and Sylvain. Rachel De Vos was also a friend. She didn't really like football and hardly came to the matches, so we often had dinners together to catch up and have our girlie talk, leaving our husbands at home to look after the kids. They were all great people and, for me, it

Partying with Ragna Hreidarsson

Going to Paris with Petra Reuser and Anne Gaardsoe

Listening to away match commentary while baking cookies with the girls

was important to have friendships that weren't based solely around football. In the players' lounge, the result always defined the mood – and rightly so – but I found it important to see people in a different environment.

While I'll always stay in touch with some of those girls, my life has undoubtedly changed in the last year, since Fab left Ipswich. In some ways, I've had to revert to a more 'boring' life. The great thing about football is that you always have that excitement of not knowing what's going to happen next. There's a lot of emotion and I used to love the drama of matches, either being there or listening to the away games on the radio (I'd always bake cookies and cakes with the girls because I wanted to listen to the commentary). I always liked being involved and, if I'm honest, I've missed that since he left Portman Road. I'll always love Ipswich and Suffolk. I made many good friends there (not just in football) and it has a special place in my heart. Our two youngest girls were born and bred there and Yasmin grew up in Ipswich.

Those years were exciting and never boring. As a wife, I had to deal with so many factors. We shared the highs (of which there were many) and I always tried to be there to comfort him through the lows (thankfully, few and far between). In many ways, I've been his manager. I'm very much a problem solver and have always dealt with things like his contracts and agents.

When you play professional football, 25,000 people have an opinion about you. Fabian was only ever bothered about two opinions - the manager's and mine. I was very critical about his football. Whenever I gave compliments he knew he'd played well, but I could also criticise him. After a game we could talk for hours about what went right or wrong, or about the system that was played. Men were often very surprised by how much I knew about football. Fabian used to come in after training and tell me about the way they trained or how much he had run. He even told me loads of things that had been said or done in the dressing room and very often I couldn't share it with the other wives.

As a footballer's wife it can be easy to lose your identity, because people know you as 'the wife of....'. However, because of my strong character I fought hard to keep my own identity and wanted to earn my own money and have my own social life. I'm happy to say I pulled it off. The great thing about us, as a couple, is that I met him when he was just starting out, still studying and only dreaming of the career he's been fortunate enough to have. I can't imagine what it must be like to date a player who's already 'made it'. Since the moment we met, Fabian has always tried to make the most of his career and I feel proud and happy to say that I've been there alongside him for the journey."

full english

looking to the future

There comes a time when you have to stop doing the things you love the most and for me, reluctantly, that means playing football. I say reluctantly because it'll be the end of a long, happy and successful era – a chapter of my life that has provided me with memories I'll cherish forever. In some ways, though, I'm ready for it and excited about new beginnings.

To be a professional footballer for nearly two decades has been fantastic but now it's time to move on. As things stand at the time of writing, I really don't know what the future holds (which is a bit scary but also exciting). However, I do know that I'd love to stay involved with the game. I've learnt so much in my time, both in terms of football and life experiences, and I'd relish the opportunity to pass that on to others.

To date, I've been offered two coaching roles (one is to be a player-coach) here in England. While it's flattering to be approached, I don't think either job is for me, mainly because it's still my intention to move back to Holland. I've been over here for 11 years and, while it's been fantastic, the time is right to head home and spend some long overdue quality time with my wonderful family – Juliette and the girls, of course, but also my mum, dad, brothers and half-sisters. There have been so many times down the years when I've had to miss out on family occasions – birthdays, parties and celebrations – and now it'll be nice to think that I can get along and be part of the fun. I've got some catching up to do.

I'm also really excited about the prospect of a normal family Christmas and New Year, rather than having to train, travel and play matches. That will be amazing, especially being able to eat and drink what I like without worrying or feeling guilty.

As I say, I really would love to stay involved with football, though, and I've got contacts at a very successful and established academy in Rotterdam. There might be a possibility of getting involved there, which would be great, and I'd love the chance to help improve young players of the future. Aside from actual football coaching, I'd enjoy just talking to them and sharing my experiences of being a pro. So many times in my career I've come across young players who think they've 'arrived' after one good game or season. However, the hard work is only just beginning and the trick, without doubt, is repeating that form over and over again. Look at top-class pros like Steven Gerrard and Frank Lampard. Both have just improved and improved and that's down to their mental approach and work-ethic. It isn't easy being a professional footballer but whatever happens, and whatever level they reach, young players should always strive to be the best they can possibly be.

In Holland there are 18 sides in the top division and 18 in the equivalent of the Championship. If you say there are about 600 players in each division, it means around 1,200 professional footballers in a country with a population of 17 million. Therefore, the chances of making the grade are very slim (especially when you consider a big chunk of that figure are foreign imports). The reason I'm saying that is not to be negative, but to make youngsters realise that they've got to stand out – both as a player and a person. And if they get a chance, they've got to grab it with both hands and hold on for dear life – because if not someone else will be ready to jump in. They have to be special and just having talent might not be enough. They have to have the drive and determination to succeed and improve.

I can put my hand on my heart and say that I've never once taken my career for granted. I was never happy after one good game or season, because if you can't repeat and sustain it people will think it was a one-off and a fluke. We've all seen it so many times, when a player with outstanding natural ability fails to make it. I saw it with my own eyes at the Ipswich academy, where some of the best players would disappear off the radar. My purpose, from now on, is to teach these young guys how to last in the jungle of professional football – it's a survival of the fittest and toughest.

Another option I've got is to work alongside my agent and very good friend Raymond van Lierop. He's looked after my interests for the last five years and, in my eyes, he's the best around because he cares about the player and his welfare – not just money (which is, of course, the stereotype of agents. I've had some who are only there to make money, constantly trying to broker and engineer transfers). It isn't about the money with Raymond, though, and that's why we've become such good friends. First and foremost, he cares about his players and what's best for them and it might be that we team up, so that I can pass on my experience and expertise. There are other things that interest me, too, like public relations and marketing. I'm very much a people person and that's definitely another area I might be tempted by.

All of these things are possibilities that excite me but, quite frankly, the first thing I'm looking forward to after the testimonial is a nice long break. I've been in football such a long time and it'll be lovely to rest and recharge my batteries.

Having said that, I know what I'm like and I'm confident I'll always train and stay fit, long after my playing days. That's just the way I am, especially having had it ingrained in me for so long. I love fitness and exercise, even if it just means roller-skating or running around the beautiful lake near our home in Rotterdam.

My other goal for the future is to run a marathon within the next two years. My old team-mates who read this will probably be very surprised or even laugh out loud, just like Simon Thadani, the fitness coach at Ipswich. I was always one of those players who never enjoyed pre-season with the sometimes cruel running exercises and tempo runs but this has become an ambition of mine over the last few years. I've always admired marathon runners and ideally I'd love to run one in my home town of Rotterdam.

I'd still love to have a kick-around from time to time, too, and nothing would give me more pleasure than representing Ipswich once again at some kind of Masters event. Who knows? It might even be something I organise and arrange myself in the future.

All in all, even though I don't know what's round the corner, I feel I've got a lot to be excited about. People have asked me if I'm daunted by the prospect of leaving my playing days behind but I'm honestly not (to be able to say that surprises me, because I always anticipated I'd feel differently).

Of course, I'm sad to some extent – I can't think of any other job that provides the same highs as scoring a goal or running out in front of a packed crowd at Portman Road. A brand new chapter of my life is about to unfold, though, and I'm happy and excited to do new things. As has always been my approach, from the early days right through my career - bring it on.

full english

First published in the
United Kingdom in 2009 by

Fabian Wilnis
11, Oak Eggar Chase
Pinewood, Ipswich
Suffolk IP8 3TE

A CIP catalogue record for this book
is available from the British Library.

ISBN 978-0-9563230-0-2

Printed and bound
in United Kingdom by

Print Wright Ltd
6 Boss Hall Business Park
Ipswich Suffolk IP1 5BN
Tel: 01473 240897